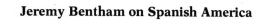

Jeremy Bentham on Spanish America

JEREMY BENTHAM ON SPANISH AMERICA

An Account of
His Letters and Proposals
to the New World

Miriam Williford

Louisiana State University Press
Baton Rouge and London

Design: Patricia Douglas Crowder
Typeface: VIP Aster
Composition: Graphic Composition, Inc.
Printing: Thomson-Shore, Inc.
Binding: John Dekker & Sons, Inc.

Grateful acknowledgment is made to the editors of *The Americas: A Quarterly Review of Inter-American Cultural History* for permission to reprint material in Chapter Six that appeared in Volume XXVII (July 1, 1970) of that periodical.

LIBRARY OF CONGRESS CATALOGING IN PUBLICATION DATA

Williford, Miriam, 1926–
    Jeremy Bentham on Spanish America.

    Bibliography: p.
    Includes index.
    1. Latin America—History—Philosophy.   2. Bentham, Jeremy, 1748–1832.   I. Title.
F1410.W574   980'.02'0924   79–25608
ISBN 0–8071–0652–6

For all who kept the faith, especially Lillie, Nick, and Connie

CONTENTS

PREFACE

THE LONG SHADOW CAST BY Jeremy Bentham over Spanish America has intrigued me for years. Struck by the many references, especially by nineteenth-century authors, to Bentham as a major influence on early Spanish American liberalism, I began to search for the nature of his influence. Finding little substantiating data in secondary works, I turned to the Bentham manuscripts at University College, London, and the British Museum. There I did not find conclusive evidence that Bentham had shaped Spanish American liberalism, but I did find a wealth of documents which indicated the scope and nature of Bentham's interest in what he termed Spanish Ultramaria.

Bentham's fascination for the area began in 1808 when he attempted to immigrate to Mexico, and it ended only with his death in 1832, when in his will he remembered José del Valle with a bequest of a ring with his picture and a lock of his hair. Bentham was well known to Spanish America largely through the French editions of his works prepared by Pierre Etienne Dumont. The concern of this study is not the impact of these printed works, however; it is instead the special laws, plans, codes, recommendations, and advice that Bentham offered through the years to Spanish America.

Many of the almost illegible documents found in the collections of University College and the British Museum have never been published and are thus largely unknown. Taken as a whole, the documents reveal Bentham's great desire to see his principles and plans put into action. Spanish America, just winning its independence, had need of advice and assistance on every level, and Jeremy Bentham, the systems maker, known to them through his works, was anxious to give them the benefit of his labors.

The emphasis of this volume then is Bentham and his interest in Spanish America. No attempt is made to determine the influence of Bentham there. Such requires extensive further research and study which, it is hoped, this work will assist and facilitate.

The Bentham manuscripts at University College, London, and the British Museum, along with John Bowring's edition of *The Works of Jeremy Bentham*, constitute the major sources for this study.

ACKNOWLEDGMENTS

MANY INSTITUTIONS AND INDIVIDUALS have aided me in this adventure. I acknowledge with gratitude and appreciation their kindness, assistance and patience. The institutions include the Co-operative Humanities Program, the Research Council of Winthrop College, the library of University College, London, the Manuscript Room of the British Museum, the library of Kings College, Cambridge, the Dacus Library of Winthrop College, and the Perkins Library of Duke University.

The list of individuals who contributed to the completion of this work is endless. But some must be mentioned. Professor Robin Humphreys of the Royal Institute of Latin American Studies was most gracious in receiving me and introducing me to others interested in Bentham. Professor J. H. Burns, Director of the Bentham Project at University College, gave me direction and encouragement. Especial thanks are due Sheila Williams and J. Percival of University College Library for their generous help in finding materials. Florence Blakeley of the Duke library always managed to locate the elusive source. Shirley Tarleton, Frances Ellison, and the entire staff of the Dacus Library gave unstinting support. Paula Treder provided much-needed encouragement and assistance throughout my Bentham research. Kudos are due Peggy Haskel and Shirley Brice Heath for their comments after reading early drafts. A special grace note is necessary for the reassurance given by my friend and colleague the late Francis Marion Nichols.

Louise Taylor, who has typed all—from the nearly illegible initial draft to the final manuscript—has my enduring respect.

Finally, I acknowledge my indebtedness to my former colleague Connie Smith Lee. Without her skill as an editor, her ability as a debater, her concern and warmth as a friend, I might have faltered along the long path between the first draft and final publication. Needless to say, I appreciate all their contributions, but the interpretations and opinions herein are mine alone.

INTRODUCTION

SPANISH AMERICA WAS TO BE Jeremy Bentham's utopia, but a utopia with a difference. Other men might create on paper the ideal society, but this would not do for a utilitarian. The ideal must become actuality. Old institutions must be destroyed, and new ones constructed based on the only valid principle, *i.e.*, the principle of utility, the greatest happiness to the greatest number. To bring about such a transformation, Spanish America would have to be freed of Spanish control, and Bentham would be necessary to direct the reconstruction that would follow. Bentham worked on every level to achieve this Spanish American independence.

But the reformation was the thing, and Bentham must be present to direct it. If Jeremy Bentham was a utilitarian, and who can doubt it, then he himself had to go to Spanish America, for here, indeed, was the utilitarian's dream: the opportunity to begin at the beginning and bring into being only those institutions, political, economic, social, which would provide the greatest happiness to the greatest number. Unfortunately, the Spanish government thwarted his plans to immigrate to Mexico and the arrest of Francisco de Miranda canceled his scheme for going to Venezuela. What would Bentham have done in Spanish America? From the evidence, he would have become their lawmaker, for Bentham believed in the total efficacy of laws; he believed that institutions and life-styles were created and molded by the proper laws. Writing of his proposed move to Venezuela, he said that he planned "to do a little business in the way of my trade . . . to draw up a body of laws for the people there . . . whatever I give them for laws, they will be prepared to receive as oracles."[1]

When his dreams of directing this regeneration in person were dashed, Bentham did not give up his desire for a utilitarian utopia in Spanish America. He simply changed his tactics. He continued to develop plans, devise schemes, and adapt others' ideas for the New World. His home became a mecca for Spanish Americans in London; he had his amanuenses scan the London press for news of Spanish America; he developed and maintained contact with Englishmen who had Spanish American interests. He bombarded Spanish American leaders with his plans for post-independence development. And, perhaps most importantly, he sought to control this development through his correspondence with these leaders. He thought they needed the benefit of his wisdom, and he generously gave this as well as sometimes vitriolic criticism. Though at times Bentham might appear superficial, vain, or even foolish, one need only read "Emancipation Spanish" (see Chapter Four herein) to discover the incisiveness of his mind and the depth and breadth of his concern for Spanish America.

With a philosophe's faith in the rationality of man, Bentham drew up proposals for a code of laws, sketched broad plans for education, designed a plan for an interoceanic canal, wrote a liberty-of-the-press law, and recommended specific governmental forms, all for Spanish America. Believing that men everywhere were alike, *i.e.*, rational, he did not bother to acquaint himself with the traditions, customs, or life-styles of the people for whom he made these plans. In actuality, he virtually ignored the existence of the indigenous peoples in Spanish America.

This New World utopia was one of the many interests of Bentham, and this interest remained more or less constant from his initial desire to immigrate in 1808 until his death in 1832. Spanish

---

1. John Bowring (ed.), *The Works of Jeremy Bentham* (11 vols.; New York, 1962), X, 457–58; hereinafter cited as *Works*.

America was to be for Bentham a proving ground for his many ideas. But perhaps more important for Bentham, the man, there, in the New World, his genius would at last be appreciated. He openly admitted this when in writing of his planned move to Venezuela, he pathetically commented, "the good which I could do to mankind if I were in the House of Commons, or even if I were minister, is inconsiderable in comparison of that which I may hope to do if I go there."[2] Bentham was to find in Spanish America, he hoped, the glory that had eluded him in his native land.

As D. J. Manning in his study *The Mind of Jeremy Bentham* points out, the failure of the ruling classes in England to accept Bentham's ideas had led him to attempt to undermine established authority and bring about "what he regarded as the inevitable recognition of his own creative genius."[3] And Spanish America was the perfect site for such an undertaking.

2. *Ibid.*
3. D. J. Manning, *The Mind of Jeremy Bentham* (London, 1968), 7.

Jeremy Bentham on Spanish America

One

WHY SPANISH AMERICA?

JEREMY BENTHAM, patriarch of the English utilitarians, showed little interest in Spanish America until 1808 when he was sixty years old. His life prior to this time falls into two rather distinct periods, the first ending with the French Revolution, the other lasting until 1810. This latter period was dominated by Bentham's struggle to make his Panopticon prison reform plan a reality.[1] Bentham had taken his master's degree from Oxford in 1766 and was called to the bar at Lincoln's Inn. The life and work of a barrister did not appeal to Bentham, however, and he soon began to devote his time to speculative thinking. In that auspicious year 1776, the year that brought to light the Declaration of Independence, Adam Smith's *The Wealth of Nations*, and Edward Gibbon's *The Decline and Fall of the Roman Empire*, Bentham published his *Fragment on Government*. And in 1789, he published his *Introduction to the Principles of Morals*. The *Fragment* and *Introduction* are unique in that they were prepared for the press by Bentham himself and not by an editor-disciple, as were most of his later works. During his early life Bentham believed that the ruling powers would recognize his

1. The definitive biography of Bentham has yet to be written. It is hoped that Professor J. H. Burns and his associates in the Bentham Project will soon fill this void. The most readable biography remains Sir Leslie Stephen's *The English Utilitarians*, Volume I. Elie Halévy's *The Growth of Philosophic Radicalism* is, of course, invaluable in understanding Bentham's thought. The biography of Bentham included by his executor, Sir John Bowring, in Bentham's *Works* is sketchy at best, distorted at times, but it is the only source for much Bentham material.

talent and so he concerned himself to a great degree with producing codes and laws that might be useful for the benevolent despots that ruled the continent of Europe. He envisioned himself as the legislator-advisor of Empress Catherine of Russia and fantasized an invitation from Louis XVI to make laws for France.[2]

But as the French Revolution toppled crowns, frightened philosophers, and changed the aspect of political problems, Bentham changed his course. While he deplored the Revolution's abstract theories of natural rights and the rights of man, he saw in the Revolution an opportune moment for putting his ideas into practice, a time for reforming legislative systems and codifying laws. He sent a part of his *Political Tactics* to France and offered to go there himself to establish a jail along the lines of his newly devised Panopticon scheme. Immediately before the Reign of Terror began, Bentham, along with others, was made an honorary citizen of France, and, when the Revolution did take its violent turn, he reacted by advising France to "Emancipate your Colonies."[3]

Meanwhile, on March 28, 1792, Bentham's father died, leaving his fairly large estate divided almost equally between his two sons, Jeremy and Samuel, a naval architect. With financial security now assured, the two brothers began in earnest to plan for the operation of the Panopticon, which was to be Bentham's masterpiece. This prison, which had as its unique quality its circular design, was according to Bentham a "mill for grinding rogues honest, and idle men industrious." In 1794 England's Parliament adopted his plan, and Bentham set about having models and architectural designs made and searching for the proper location for the prison. While Parliament debated his plan for prisons, Bentham hit upon the idea of using the system to solve the growing problem of pauperism as well. Though Bentham worked furiously, expending huge sums of his own, the final warrant for the construction money never came. Bentham suffered sorely from this defeat and blamed the personal animosity of George III for the cancellation of his prison plans. Slowly, however, he recovered from the hu-

2. Elie Halévy, *The Growth of Philosophic Radicalism* (Boston, 1966), 150.
3. This was not published, however, at this time. Leslie Stephen, *The English Utilitarians* (3 vols.; New York, 1968 [1900]), I, 198.

miliation that he felt because his scheme failed to become reality. As Sir Leslie Stephen so aptly described Bentham's meditation on the Panopticon fiasco, he "had at last found out that he had begun at the wrong end." He began to understand that, indeed, governments as then organized did *not* want to provide the greatest happiness to the greatest number. With this realization he ceased his efforts for piecemeal reform and concentrated instead on how a government could be so constructed that its primary concern was the creation of the greatest happiness for the greatest number. From this time on, he became involved in the overall problems of political organization rather than just in penal codes and other particular reforms.[4]

Bentham himself says that he had come to such conclusions at some point before 1809. Perhaps not accidentally, then, it was in 1808 that his first evidence of interest in Spanish America appeared. This concern for Spanish America was precipitated by a North American, Aaron Burr, whom Bentham's biographer Sir Leslie Stephen described as "the strange adventurer, politician, lawyer, and filibuster, famous for the deed in which he killed Alexander Hamilton, and now framing wild schemes for an empire in Mexico." Burr evidently came to the attention of Bentham through the good offices of Etienne Dumont, Bentham's editor for French editions of his work, who wrote to Bentham that he had met a "Mr. Edward in England; in America, it was Mr. Burr" who upon hearing Dumont's name asked if he "were the person to whom he was indebted for his acquaintance with the writings of Bentham." Burr, perhaps realizing Bentham's weakness for flattery, said that his writings made Montesquieu's seem trifling, and he "was anxiously desirous of knowing the author,—of passing a day with him: this, said he, would be a satisfaction for the rest of his life." Dumont then assured Bentham that he would not be sorry if he issued Burr such an invitation, for in spite of what Bentham might think of the Hamilton affair, "he has no desire whatever to break your head."[5]

4. *Ibid.*, 200, 213–214; Bowring (ed.), *Works*, X, 226.
5. Bowring (ed.), *Works*, III, 435, and V, 278; Stephen, *The English Utilitarians*, I, 220; Bowring (ed.), *Works*, X, 433.

Bentham immediately tendered the invitation, and Burr's *Journal* contains the entry "1808, August 11. Received invitation from Jeremy Bentham inviting me to pass some days *chez lui*." Bentham at this time was staying at his country place, Barrow Green, and for August 18, 19, and 20, Burr joined him there. Upon his return to London, Bentham's hospitality continued as Burr took up lodgings on August 22 at Bentham's Queen Square Place, a practice he continued from time to time whether Bentham was in residence there or not. It is a pity that no record exists of the conversations that went on between these two during these visits. Burr was still hopeful of carrying his Mexican dreams into reality and evidently talked enthusiastically with Bentham about them. It was perhaps while listening to Burr as he talked of his plans for Mexico that Bentham first saw the possibilities of Spanish America as the testing ground for utilitarian ideas. In what was a reminiscence of Burr addressed to John Bowring decades later, Bentham stated, "He (Burr) came here expecting this government to assist his endeavours in Mexico; but the government had just then made up their quarrel with Spain. . . . He meant really to make himself Emperor of Mexico. He told me, I should be the legislator, and he would send a ship of war for me. . . . He said, the Mexicans would all follow, like a flock of sheep."[6]

Bentham was intrigued by the talk of Mexico. And though Burr had failed to get support for his Mexican scheme, he had succeeded in creating in Bentham Mexican designs of his own, for Bentham immediately began to make plans to immigrate to Mexico. He realized that he had to have the permission of the Spanish government for such a move and that his interest in Mexico must seem to be purely academic and not at all political or revolutionary. Thus in a long letter dated October 31, 1808, Bentham asked the assistance of the British Ambassador to Spain, Henry Richard Vassal Fox, Lord Holland, in gaining the permission of the Spanish government to go to Mexico to live. Bentham requested that Lord Holland recommend him to his Lordship's

6. Matthew L. Davis (ed.), *The Private Journal of Aaron Burr* (2 vols.; New York, 1838), I, 27–28; Bowring (ed.), *Works*, X, 432.

friend, Gaspar de Jovellanos, and give to this Spanish minister of justice "a certificate of harmlessness" certifying that Bentham was disqualified "in all points for everything that, in French, is called, *Intrigue*, or in the English, *politics*." Such a statement, this "*certificate of nothingness*" was the "best recommendation that, on a visit to Mexico, a man could carry in his pocket." For permission to go to Mexico, Bentham would promise Jovellanos "to persevere in support of the principle of *Laissez nous faire*, so long as I have the stump of a pen left." Jovellanos, he suspected, had probably heard of him through Dumont's works, 750 copies of which had found their way to the peninsula. He also reminded Lord Holland that his request to go would not be the first such since Baron von Humboldt had been allowed to go and write what he pleased. "The favour thus granted a Frenchman, would not at this time be refused an Englishman."[7]

For any such assistance that Lord Holland might give, Bentham wondered if "a feather or two from the crown of Montezuma, if there should happen to be such a thing left" might please Lady Holland. And Bentham promised to send to Holland House copies of all Mexican poetry ever printed so that it might be translated by his Lordship into "elegant English." Here, Bentham revealed a bit of his wit: "But, Sir, Oh, yes, my lord, I know the difference. *Prose* is where all the lines but the last go on to the Margin—*poetry* is where some of them fall short of it."

Returning to his main objective Bentham continued on to say that, should Jovellanos require a trip to Spain for a personal interview before giving approval, then, much as he disliked the idea "it should not be shrunk from." He hoped, however, to be allowed to sail directly from England, but he was quite concerned about getting from the port of Veracruz to Mexico City without delay. In his usual classifying manner, Bentham listed for his friend those documents which he considered indispensable for his trip. First, a letter from Spain to the viceroy of Mexico recommending Bentham to his protection so long as he was on his good behavior and

7. Surely Bentham knew that Humboldt was not French! Bowring (ed.), *Works*, X, 439–44.

a similar letter to the governor of Veracruz requesting him to allow Bentham to move through the port city without having to stay overnight or at most a single night.

So much for the mandatory items. Other desirable concessions from the Spanish minister included exemption from baggage search at Veracruz, although it would be acceptable in Mexico City where the climate was better and the inspectors were presumably more sophisticated. In addition to these requests, he asked Lord Holland for information about packetboats or other ships traveling from Spain to Veracruz; for a copy of the *Index Expurgatorius* to ensure he did not unintentionally violate it; for a map of Mexico showing roads, if possible; and for books telling of prices, goods, and services available in Mexico. While all this information would make his planning easier, Bentham stressed that these requests should not in any way delay or prevent the achievement of the two indispensable letters.

Bentham stated that to facilitate matters he was sending the letter in an amanuensis's hand while reserving his almost illegible hand for verification of the letter's authenticity. A postscript added his plans to take with him Mr. John Herbert Koe of Lincoln's Inn and one or two servants if permitted.[8]

With his request made, Bentham continued to make his plans. In a letter to his cousin, Dr. J. Mulford, dated just eight days after the one to Holland, he told of his plans to immigrate, the reasons for his decision, and the means he was using to gain permission. He was not, however, unaware of the unrest that was beginning to pervade the Spanish empire. He very openly wondered how long Mexico would remain a colony of Spain. This would not mean a change in his plans because "to submit to be governed by them [the Spanish] is *one thing*; to receive a man civilly, who comes with a letter of recommendation from them is another."[9]

Bentham concluded his letter by saying that he was studying manuscript road maps and reading unpublished journals of travels between Veracruz and Mexico. Perhaps this was the source for

8. *Ibid.*
9. *Ibid.*, 444–46.

the document in the University College London collection that gives the distance from Mexico City to Veracruz by listing the number of leagues from the capital to the first town and so on through twenty-nine such stops, ending with Veracruz. In Bentham's own hand on this sheet are questions such as the length of the league, which road the carriage takes, when the map was published, from whom it was obtained, and what defense there was, if any, against bugs. Then he listed some information about sailing and ships and the number of days by ship from Jamaica to Veracruz.[10]

Such evidence of the seriousness of Bentham's desire to go to Mexico abounds. Bentham had copied from the *Almanak Mercantil y Guía de Commerciantes para el año de 1806*, published at Madrid, the names of the members and employees of the consulados of Mexico and Veracruz; the merchants of those two cities as well as those of Xalapa, brokers, and other attorneys and officials whose major concern was commerce. In addition he had in Spanish from the *Guía* information concerning the postal service there.

From Bentham's inquiring, classifying mind came also a list of some forty-five questions about Mexico and life there. The range and detail of these questions indicate much about Bentham and his priorities. The list includes queries about the use, availability, source, and price of candles and writing paper; the existence of libraries, botanical gardens, French and English books, books and maps of Mexico, physicians (especially Irish), printers, engravers, sculptors, architects, tea, and, if tea was available, if teapots and milk were used; the obligation of going to mass and confession; the status of women, when they married, when they ceased childbearing, and if their husbands were jealous; and finally travel, the distances between Veracruz and the capital and the types of carriages available. One amusing question reveals Bentham's need for a map of Mexico: he wondered if he would dock at the port of Veracruz or Acapulco!

Bentham also clipped articles containing information about

10. Undated notes, in Bentham Papers, University College, London, LX, 6–11; hereinafter cited as UCL.

Mexico from the London newspapers. These concerned Mexico's adherence to Ferdinand VII and thus the Cortes of Cádiz, her contributions to the war effort against the Napoleons, and, most important perhaps for Bentham, a notice from the *Times* of February 29, 1809: "on the 1st of Feb. the Justo arrived at Cádiz, her voyage from Veracruz was made in 56 days."

In time Bentham learned that Lord Holland had arrived at Corunna, Spain, and he was assured by a footman at Holland House on November 14 that a packet of letters was to leave for Spain and Lord Holland the following day and that his letter would be included.[11]

As he awaited some response from Lord Holland, he persisted in his search for information about Mexico. Francis Horner gave him a few more facts about Mexico but largely in the form of critical analyses of various sources on it. He mentioned M. Thierry, Arrowsmith's map, Pinkerton's *Geography*, and Alcedos' *Dictionary*. He also answered a question asked him by John Herbert Koe, the proposed traveling companion, concerning attempts to transfer the insect cochineal to India. Horner reported that, while efforts had been made, none had achieved total success, but a reward was still outstanding "to anyone who will carry out the true insect to India."[12]

Bentham's first response to his request came from Lord Holland at Seville in a letter dated February 18, 1809. Although Lord Holland could give Bentham no firm answer, he informed his fellow countryman that he had given his petition to Jovellanos who "espoused your cause most eagerly, as he is not unacquainted with your character, acquirements and merits." He cautioned Bentham, however, that though Jovellanos was the leading man in the Spanish government, "there is, unfortunately, so little of a *lead* in the Government here." Consequently, on his advice, Lord Holland had prepared a petition in Bentham's name, which Jovellanos himself had kindly drawn up, and submitted it to the government.

11. *Ibid.*
12. Cochineal, native to Mexico and Central America, was a major source of red dye for textiles. Bowring (ed.), *Works*, X, 446–47.

The petition, Bentham was told, had played down Bentham as a "Jurisconsultus" and writer of criminal law, making them seem only accidental, while making the request on the basis of Bentham's love of botany, antiquities, and his precarious health. Lord Holland apologized for such emphases but explained that he thought that they strengthened his case.[13]

The final word came from Jovellanos himself, accompanied by a note from Lord Holland. Jovellanos began by assuring Bentham of his desire to help him in every way possible, but his letter reveals his awareness of the delicacy of Bentham's request. His petition to go to Mexico directly from England, Jovellanos wrote, might present difficulties which could be eliminated if he would come to Cádiz and "se expusiere por motivo de ella cualquier objeto de observacion y estudio relativo a la historia natural o á ciencios fisicas." But the special treatment Bentham had requested at Veracruz could not be granted, though the Spanish authorities would recommend the official proceedings be as brief as possible. In spite of the friendly, warm tone of Jovellanos' letter, it revealed a nagging concern over allowing Bentham access to Mexico. After explaining that certain formalities would be necessary in Mexico City for Bentham to have the liberty he chose, Jovellanos pointedly explained that whereas the Spanish government wanted to study the established law of Mexico, it could not at that time be changed. Perhaps realizing that this would be Bentham's major concern in Mexico, Jovellanos concluded by recommending that Bentham give up his plans to go to Mexico because "time and circumstances do not appear to me to promise you that tranquil security you seek." If Bentham persisted in his desire, however, then Jovellanos promised him his every assistance. One wonders at this point if Jovellanos really feared for the safety of Bentham or for the safety of Mexico as a Spanish colony with Bentham living there.[14]

Lord Holland's accompanying letter from Holland House

13. *Ibid.,* 447.
14. *Ibid.,* 448. The Spanish original is found in Cándido Nocedal *et al.* (eds.), *Obras de Don Gaspar Melchor de Jovellanos* (3 vols.; Madrid, 1858–1956), II, 319–20.

seemed to assume that Bentham would still carry forward his plans. He advised Bentham that he might go to Seville any time after the present month "with perfect security from agues" if the French didn't get there first. But he made no recommendation himself that Bentham proceed to do so. He informed his friend that a free constitution was being drawn up in Seville at that time and that Jovellanos was dedicating all his time and efforts to that. Had Bentham gone to Seville, would he have gone on to Mexico or would he have been too intrigued by the work of the framers of the new constitution to want to leave that opportunity?[15]

In spite of Jovellanos' advice and the critical situation in Spain, Bentham did not immediately give up thinking about Mexico. In a letter on April 24, 1810, to his cousin, Dr. Mulford, he told of his near neighbor, Cochran Johnson, who had indeed been to Mexico and told tales of it that he could hardly believe, about the size of the flowers, the animals, and the plants, and the blending of the races, white, red, and black. Of the latter, Bentham had seen an oil painting of the results which astounded him. In addition he told Mulford that his neighbor had a magnificent map of Mexico City, the first ever in Britain.[16]

While waiting for Jovellanos' letter, Bentham had made contact with a Spanish American who was to change his desired destination. When Bentham met General Francisco de Miranda is uncertain. W. S. Robertson states that Bentham was one of those calling on Miranda as early as 1785. Yet there is no evidence that Miranda had stirred Bentham's interest in Spanish America prior to his meeting Burr. In the *Archivo del General Miranda* appears a note from Mr. Koe returning to him the Caracas *Gazette* along with some of Bentham's unpublished works. Mr. Bentham, it stated, "would feel himself much obliged" if the general would send by the bearer of the note the map of America by Faden, the almanac of Mexico, and Pages' *Journey from New Orleans to Mexico*. This

---

15. Bowring (ed.), *Works*, X, 448, 477. In December of 1813 Lord Holland sent Bentham a small bust of Jovellanos, who had been murdered in 1812. Bentham received the bust with gratitude and gave it the best position in his workshop.

16. *Ibid.*, 455.

note is dated February 3, 1808. Evidently Miranda complied with the request and probably talked with Bentham about his plans because another note dated 1809 accompanied the return of "the Map of Colombia—Dupons—the map of Mexico and the Mexican Guide" and asked Miranda for the return of Bentham's book by Jovellanos. This guide was probably the *Guia de Commerciantes* from which Bentham made his notes.[17]

Sometime in 1808 Bentham met James Mill, historian, economist, and father of John Stuart Mill, who for many years thereafter worked closely with Bentham as an editor. Mill became the go-between and actually the better friend of Miranda. On August 25, 1809, Bentham wrote Miranda a brief letter telling him that he had commissioned Mill to invite him to visit them at Barrow Green House. Mill complied, telling the general of the desire of Koe, Bentham, and Mrs. Mill for his acceptance of the invitation, promising rest, rustic hospitality, his own services as his secretary if needed, and pointing out the nearness (only three hours) to London if his presence was required there. He told him, too, "You will see the Edin. Review, if you come here . . . our article is there." Miranda, however, refused this invitation.[18]

But evidently at some time Miranda did see Bentham, for in another letter to his cousin Mulford, this one dated November, 1810, Bentham wrote, "You mention Mexico. Mexico I have no longer any thoughts of. But another country still more charming, the province of Venezuela, *alias* the Caracas, so called from the capital, I have serious thoughts of." Although he explained his change of plans first by describing the abundant rains and rivers in Venezuela, the summer temperature the year round, and the sight of the sea and ice-capped mountains, he confessed that he had other more significant motives for going to Venezuela. It was

17. Miranda Papers, Vol. 7, as cited in William Spence Robertson, *The Life of Miranda* (2 vols.; Chapel Hill, 1929), I, 62; Vicente Dávila *et al.* (eds.), *Archivo del General Miranda* (24 vols.; La Habana, 1929–1950), XXI, 54; XXII, 256.

18. Dávila *et al.* (eds.), *Archivo del General Miranda*, XXIII, 52–54. The article referred to is the review of "Lettre aux Espanols Americains, Par un de leur Compatriotes," which they had collaborated on for the *Edinburgh Review*, XIII (October, 1808–January, 1809), 277–311. See Robertson, *The Life of Miranda*, II, 48–53, 59, 57–58, and Chapter Six herein.

here that he admitted his desire "to do a little business in the way of my trade—to draw up a body of laws for the people there, they having, together with a number of the other Spanish American colonies, taken advantage of the times, and shaken off the Spanish yoke, which was a very oppressive one."[19]

Bentham identified Miranda as having dedicated his life to the emancipation of the Spanish colonies. The general, Bentham reported, had left England just two weeks before "by invitation to put himself at the head of them." Miranda had taken with him a draft of a law for liberty of the press that Bentham had drawn up for him.[20] Bentham explained further that Miranda would write to him immediately after he arrived and, if things were peaceful, Bentham planned "to take a trip there not long after I have received his letter." He stressed the seriousness of his intentions to go. "I see nothing that can prevent my going if I am alive and well" except Venezuelan confusion or Miranda's losing ascendancy, "which there can be no doubt of his possessing at present there." But Bentham saw no indication that either of those things would occur.

Indeed, others planned or at least wanted to go to Venezuela, especially Lady Hester Stanhope, William Pitt's niece, who promised Miranda, if all things went well for him there, to go and "superintend female schools for him. . . . Even William Wilberforce, who gave them an entertainment t'other day, talked, half jest, half earnest, of paying them a visit."[21]

It was in this letter to his cousin Mulford that he boasted of the good that he could do mankind if he went to Venezuela. He continued, that, indeed, "when I am just ready to drop into the grave, my fame has spread itself all over the civilized world and by a selection only that was made A.D. 1802, from my papers, by a friend, and published at Paris, I am considered as having superceded everything that was written before me on the subject of legislation."[22]

19. Bowring (ed.), *Works*, X, 457–58.
20. See Chapter V herein.
21. Bowring (ed.), *Works*, X, 457–58.
22. *Ibid.*

Miranda did keep in touch with Bentham after his arrival in Venezuela. Here is a brief letter to Bentham dated Head Quarters, Maracay, June 2, 1812.

My Dear Sir, —I hope the day is not far distant, when I shall see the liberty and happiness of this country established upon a solid and permanent footing. The appointment I have just received, of Generalissimo of the Confederation of Venezuela, with full powers to treat with foreign nations, &c., will perhaps facilitate the means of promoting the object I have for so many years had in view. MIRANDA.[23]

Does this imply that soon he expected to invite Bentham to come to Venezuela? It is impossible to say, for at the end of the following month Miranda himself was accused of treason by some of his own Venezuelan officers. Soon he was in the hands of the Spanish and in the latter part of 1813 he was moved to a prison at Cádiz.[24] Whether he communicated with Bentham after the above letter is not known. No correspondence between the two appears in collections of the British Museum or University College, London. The next mention of Miranda by Bowring was a notice of his death dated July 14, 1816. Whether this notice from a servant of the former generalissimo was a personal note to Bentham or a statement from the press is not revealed.[25]

With the failure of Miranda, Bentham forever gave up his plans for immigration to Spanish America. But Spanish America remained a focal point for utilitarian design. As it became increasingly evident that Spanish America was destined to become independent, Bentham determined that this area should not be deprived of his ideas, thoughts, and plans even if he were not present to implement them. In his mind these new republics, angry

23. *Ibid.*, 468.
24. See Robertson, *The Life of Miranda*, II, 167–215.
25. The announcement in its entirety reads: "This day, at five minutes past one in the morning, my beloved master, Don Francisco de Miranda, resigned his spirit to the Creator; the curates and monks would not allow me to give him any funeral rites; therefore, in the same state in which he expired, with mattress, sheets, and other bedclothes, they seized hold of him and carried him away for interment, they immediately afterwards came and took away his clothes, and everything belonging to him, to burn them." Bowring (ed.), *Works*, X, 487–88.

and disillusioned with the institutions brought over from Spain, needed and indeed would welcome assistance in the creation of new governments and institutions—those based on the only proper principle, that of providing the greatest happiness to the greatest number. To ensure such an outcome and to assist in it, Bentham corresponded with Spanish American leaders. Some letters, though never posted, were kept in his records. He maintained a lengthy correspondence with only three, namely, Bernardino Rivadavia of Buenos Aires, Simón Bolívar of Colombia, and José del Valle of Guatemala. In addition he drew up plans, codes, outlines, laws to guide one and all in these heady days of freedom and independence. He carefully scanned the London papers, particularly the *Morning Chronicle*, for all Latin American news. He maintained correspondence with Englishmen abroad and those planning to make the journey to the New World. He boasted once of his having correspondents in Chile, Buenos Aires, Peru, Mexico, and Colombia.[26] His Queen Square home became a magnet for visiting Spanish Americans in London. In addition to all this activity he found time to develop an old idea along new lines as he wrote and rewrote long letters to the Spanish people pointing out the futility and illegality of their keeping America in subjection.

From the mass of Bentham's Spanish American documents— the letters, codes, laws, plans—emerges in a fairly broad outline Bentham's ideas of colonies, government, the code, education, the press, as well as many other minor ideas. For the most part these were written during the last decade and a half of his life; thus, they may be fairly revealing of the thoughts of the older Bentham. These documents are, in the main, largely unpublished ones. They are then the pure Bentham, the unedited Bentham, that is, Bentham without the modifications of editor-disciples such as Dumont, Mill, Austin, or Bowring. More important, however, taken as a whole they probably reveal the pattern of development that Bentham saw as the most efficacious for Spanish America, the design that he would have carried out had he been able to construct his New World utopia.

26. Bentham to Bernardino Rivadavia, June 13 and 15, 1822, in UCL, XII, 387.

Two

THE CODE

ELIE HALÉVY DESCRIBED BENTHAM as being "possessed by one fixed idea: to secure the drawing up and promulgation of his entire Code, everywhere, somewhere, no matter where."[1] Indeed, it had been the very nature of English common law that had so frustrated his work as a barrister that he gave it up. The one recurring interest throughout Bentham's life is this intense desire to see the law of a land not only written but complete and systematized. If a nation had a proper code, Bentham believed, then its development along utilitarian lines became virtually perfunctory. The code then was the focal point for the creation of a utilitarian state. Bentham saw himself as the one person by training, background, philosophy, and ability uniquely qualified to draw up such an all comprehensive code. Throughout his adult life Bentham sought invitations to put these qualifications to use in drawing up codes for any country, anywhere. Not surprisingly then, from the time Bentham became interested in Spanish America the code and its adoption seem to be his principal concern in Spanish America.

Bentham had fantasized that Burr would make him legislator of Mexico. When all plans for immigration to Mexico failed, Bentham began writing proposals for Spanish America arguing the need for a comprehensive code. Much of his correspondence with Spanish American leaders dealt with the necessity of such a code. Finally in 1822, he reduced all of his arguments to a single state-

1. Halévy, *The Growth of Philosophic Radicalism*, 149.

ment entitled *Codification Proposal*, which he had printed and distributed widely.[2] The evident purpose of this document was to ad-
vertise Bentham's availability as a codifier and the advantages of
accepting Bentham's offer. The proposal argued for an all-comprehensive code, based on a rationale that supported the greatest
happiness principle. This code should be drawn up by a single person whose identity was known, preferably a foreigner who had the
appropriate aptitude—*i.e.*, Bentham. Later Bentham published a
supplement to his *Proposal* composed of testimonials to his "appropriate aptitude" from important political figures in England,
Geneva, Spain, Portugal, Italy, France, United States, Greece, and
South America. For the South American testimonials Bentham
used letters from Rivadavia and del Valle.

Bentham had this *Codification Proposal* translated into Spanish
and sent copies to his Spanish American correspondents. But with
Spanish America, whether he used the formal proposal or not,
Bentham never dealt with the code substantively. Rather both in
the *Proposal* and in his letters, he argued the need of the code, his
capability in drawing it up, and the past success and acceptance
of his work with it.

Before printing this *Proposal*, however, Bentham had written a
number of plans for codification. He had turned his mind to immigration to Venezuela when his Mexican plans failed to mater-
ialize. In Bentham's manuscripts at University College, London,
are two documents prepared for Miranda in August of 1810, two
months before Miranda left on his ill-fated expedition. Whether
copies of these drafts ever reached the Venezuelan is not known.
However, they indicate the nature of Bentham's thought about
Spanish America and the code. Here then can be seen in part what
Bentham thought must be done to make Spanish America into
strong, functioning utilitarian states. As well, these documents
constitute the earliest statement of his views about this area and
its particular needs and lay out general patterns which he continued to develop until his death.

2. Jeremy Bentham, *Codification Proposal, addressed by Jeremy Bentham to all
Nations Professing Liberal Opinions* (London, 1822).

The first document is headed "Caracas Necessity of an all-comprehensive code." It reads as a preface or preamble to such a code. Beginning with the subtitle "Necessity of an entire new body of law for Venezuela," Bentham argued that the necessity was too evident to need dwelling upon. The Spanish body of laws he described as "shapeless and confused, redundant and deficient at the same time." He continued by arguing, "No intelligent Spaniard could take it in hand without seeing abundant reason for wishing to see it replaced even in Spain and for the use of Spain by an entire body of law dictated by a degree of intelligence corresponding in sure degree to that which at present manifests itself in every other walk of society." This new code, Bentham declared, must adhere to the fundamental utilitarian principle of providing the greatest happiness to the greatest number. It must "fulfill . . . the purpose professed by every body of laws even that of providing . . . the best possible means for the welfare of the people."[3] As Halévy describes Bentham's passion for codification, "The code, the systematic collection of all the laws, is called upon to become the universal manual of utilitarian morality."[4]

In addition this code must be simply written so that every citizen might understand it. Illustrative of this is Bentham's statement in this document that, "In the case of each individual the burthen imposed by it upon his attention and his memory may be as light as possible:—so that no man may either be punished or debarred of his right through ignorance."[5]

Following these three manuscript pages is a fourth in the same handwriting, undated, with the heading "paragraph 8. Prospect of adoption by other states." This document clearly illustrates that Bentham was concerned not only with Venezuela but with all Spanish America. He hoped to use Venezuela as the starting point in his plan to reshape all of Spanish America into utilitarian states. In this draft Bentham began the offer to draw up a code of

3. "Caracas Necessity of an all Comprehensive Code," 1810, in UCL, XII, 1, 2. (For the sake of consistency I am correcting the spellings of place names in Bentham's titles.)

4. Halévy, *The Growth of Philosophic Radicalism*, 78.

5. "Caracas Necessity of Code," 1810, p. 3.

laws for Venezuela which could serve as a model for other Spanish American states:

> If this foreigner should be engaged to draw up a compleat body of laws for Venezuela, and if having been established as such in Venezuela, the execution of the work should stand the test of experience, it would stand no inconsiderable chance of being adopted in other free states formed out of the Spanish settlements in America. The possession of a common body of laws would thus find all of them a bond of union, and a common convenience which to Venezuela alone would belong the glory of the example.

He stressed the advantage of such "an inter-community of laws" which would allow the use of the same judges by the several states because impartiality could thus be assured.

Having Bentham draw up the code would prevent any animosity on the part of other nations, he promised, because "in taking thus its laws from a sister state each might [have] in a sort of national pride a principle of reluctance which would have no place in the case of a body of laws drawn up by hand alike foreign to them all." This theme of the relative advantage rather than handicap of having a foreigner draw up a nation's code appears again and again in Bentham's Spanish American work.[6]

In the second, rather strange document entitled "Intended for Caracas on the occasion of General Miranda's expedition," Bentham outlined numerous suggestions and needs of Venezuela and showed in bold relief the type of action he would take once he had arrived in Venezuela. Among these, once more, he pointed out the need for codification: "In statute laws such root (of uncertainty in law or fact) can hardly have place unless in a Code self declared all comprehensive: because without such declaration unwritten law fills up all vacuities." Bentham again attempted to convince Miranda of the need to change from the old Spanish system to his new one. Bentham listed the possible evils of such a move and then told of safeguards and protection from these evils. Outlining the evils as changes in penal, non-penal, and constitutional sys-

6. *Ibid.*, 4.

tems, Bentham promised that in the penal system the accused would be allowed a choice of the old or new systems; in non-penal no changes in contracts or conveyances would be allowed that would not have been legal under the old; but in the constitutional system the loss of emoluments or power attached to office would be different. "All public power being but a trust; benefit of people the object, no satisfaction for it *as such* can be due." Bentham did suggest, however, that salaries of such discontinued offices be continued if the official could not be moved to another position. But all of these changes would be worthwhile because "in none of the established systems has the state of effect in human feeling been the object/the standard of regard. The imagination/fancy alone not the heart in any case has been consulted/case not yet the judgement by lawyers/men of law, in the formation of their rules."[7]

In a third document, entitled "J. B.'s [illeg] for Caracas Code Venezuela," written between August 15, 1810, and September 9, 1810, Bentham continued these same arguments but devoted more time to convincing the Caracans that he, Jeremy Bentham, should be the foreigner to draw up their code. He referred them to Dumont's translation of his work for confirmation of his ability; he argued again the validity of a foreigner, singlehandedly, drawing up the code. Then he launched into a long autobiographical section called "J. B. advantages derived from English birth and Education" in which he stressed the value of experience in English law for any code maker. "England is the country the jurisprudence of which compared with that of any other country affords beyond comparison the richest of materials for the use of the legislator." This, he continued, was true because England had such vast quantities of statute law and an immense stock of decisions and the state of the law was nowhere on such a bad footing as in England due to its system of common law rather than a code. Bentham moved then to a most obvious objection to his drawing up the

7. "J. B.'s [illeg.] for Caracas Code Venezuela," 1810, in UCL, XXI, 57–76, 59, 12, 71. Bentham labored to use the most appropriate word. His manuscripts are filled with duplicates where Bentham had not decided on the exact shade of meaning. These are quoted as above with the word appearing above the line always following the diagonal.

code, religion. Relying again on his English background, he argued that "though attached to its own religion, the English Government had never in its dealings with foreign nations applied itself to gaining proselytes." This, he pointed out, had always been true in regard to Catholics within Canada and the French West Indies. Even, he continued, Hindus and Mohammedans in India have been left to their own faiths by the government, while zealous individuals who sought their conversion to Christianity have been discouraged rather than encouraged by the government. He emphasized his own attitude, "To Mr. B. of all Englishmen no such wish could ever occur as that of sacrificing to the interests of the religion under which it happened to him to be born and bred, those of any other nation with whom it might happen to have to do."[8]

When it became evident to Bentham that he would never be able to go to Spanish America and personally supervise its development, he felt that he could perchance still shape their destiny through recommendations and suggestions given in person and by letter and through Englishmen who were fortunate enough to succeed in going to Spanish America. Bernardino Rivadavia appears to be the next Spanish American after Miranda to pique the interest of Bentham. Bentham had met the Argentine through a Chilean agent in England, Antonio Alvarez de Jonte, while he was on a diplomatic effort to Europe around 1817 or 1818. He entertained Rivadavia in his Queen Square home and corresponded with him upon his return to Paris and then to Buenos Aires.

Rivadavia, probably more than any other Spanish American, was a disciple of Bentham, and in his brief tenure as minister of government in the State of Buenos Aires in the early twenties his policies reflected this. Bentham proudly followed his reform program through the *Morning Chronicle* and continued his correspondence. In a letter dated April 5, 1824, he boasted to Rivadavia that William E. Laurence had stopped over in Rio and that the minister at Rio "had over and over again pledged himself to propose at

8. *Ibid.*, 3–6.

the meeting of the Cortes that I should be invited to draw up a compleat body of laws for them." It was Bentham's *Codification Proposal*, however, that caused him to write a somewhat scathing letter to Rivadavia. In this same letter of April 5, Bentham congratulated Rivadavia on his statesmanship, but he continued, "never has the pleasure produced by these cheering accounts been unalloyed, accompanied as it has been with the idea of having been cast off by a disciple, if I may take the liberty of calling you so, of whom I have so much reason to be proud." A copy of a letter from James Bevans in Buenos Aires had fallen into Bentham's hands. This letter reported that one of Bentham's works was being denounced in Buenos Aires as unintelligible. While Bentham evidently had little respect for the informer Bevans, he hastened to explain to Rivadavia that if it was the *Propuesta de Codigo*, the Spanish translation of his *Codification Proposal*, he would not be surprised if the translation was unintelligible because he had heard from others that it was full of misconceptions. These were due, however, to the haste with which the translator, a Spanish priest, had had to work, and W. E. Laurence, who knew both the work and the priest well, acknowledged the errors.[9]

Bentham continued to use this Spanish translation, however. In a letter to Simon Bolívar dated July 14, 1825, Bentham told the Liberator he was sending him copies of this *Codification Proposal*, but he added, "The translation is by Spaniards said to be extremely erroneous and inadequate. It was made up in great haste by a person who either was born in Peru or had been there and who thought he spoke fairly good English, [and] fairly acknowledged . . . his own inaptitude with reference to such a subject." To overcome these handicaps, Bentham included copies of the *Proposal* in English as well.[10]

In none of the Bentham documents that treat Spanish America and the code did Bentham concern himself with the particular economic, social, geographic, or political conditions that might be determining factors in the drawing up of fundamental codes. Ben-

9. Bentham to Rivadavia, April 5, 1824, in UCL, XII, 270–72.
10. *Ibid.*, 336.

tham throughout held to the opinion that a comprehensive code that was excellent for one state would be excellent for any other state no matter what the difference in tradition or condition. While he was aware of national differences, he believed national circumstance and character to be modifiable by the introduction of useful institutions; and his code would create those.[11]

Illustrative of Bentham's attitude concerning the universality of the applicability of his codes is a document headed "1821 Proposed Letter from J. B. to O'Higgins Supreme Director of Chile Not sent being superceded May 1822 by the printed Codification Proposal." This seven-page letter "has for its principal object the respectful tender of my services, such as they are, in the character of Draughtsman for the preparation of a Code of Law—I mean an all-comprehensive Code for the territory over the destinies of which you preside." Bentham assured the director that he understood the gravity of his suggestion and the necessity of proving himself worthy of the task. Since his written work was too voluminous to be sent to Chile, Bentham offered testimonials witnessing to his appropriate aptitude for such an undertaking. These were to include statements from the governments of Spain, Portugal, and Geneva, from "distinguished Functionaries of the Anglo-American United States," from Emperor Alexander of Russia, from the draughtsmen who drew up the Napoleonic Code of France, and the Frenchmen who drew up the Code of Penal Law for Bavaria, and finally one from the English government. Most of these testimonials finally became a part of the printed *Proposal.* Bentham hastened to explain that while the testimonials from Spain were included, they in no way contradicted his friendship for Spanish America. Here again he told of his attempts to persuade Spain of the efficacy of giving up her empire. His soon-to-be-published *Rid Yourselves of Ultramaria* would, he thought, convince O'Higgins of the validity of his friendship for both Spain and Spanish America.[12]

11. See Stephen, *The English Utilitarians*, I, 282, 7.
12. Bentham to Bernardo O'Higgins, 1821, in UCL, LX, 66–67. See Chapter Four herein.

Bentham discussed at length the most evident objection to his drawing up Chile's basic code, "the notion of incompetency—radical and incurable incompetency—on the part of every foreigner, as such, with reference to such a work." Actually, Bentham continued, "so far from affording any the slightest presumption of incompetency, this very circumstance has presented itself to *me* as being, all other circumstances equal, an efficient cause of superior aptitude." For proof he stressed that he would not use historical precedents such as ancient Rome's mission to Athens which resulted in the Ten Tables or the medieval Italian republics' habit of resorting to each other for a magistrate. He promised O'Higgins instead to include in the letter a paper which told how he reached the decision that a foreigner was better than a native as codifier.[13]

About the same time he was writing to O'Higgins, Bentham wrote an outline for a constitutional code for Colombia. This one-page document is dated May 30, 1822, and headed "Columbia Constitutional Code A 1821 Titles and Sections." To whom, if anyone it was sent is not known. Bentham divided this into ten divisions: the first concerned the nation; the second, the government and territory; the third, the parochial and electoral assemblies; the fourth, legislative power; the fifth, executive power; the sixth, judicial power; the seventh, the interior organization of the republic; the eighth, general dispositions; the ninth, the oath of office; the tenth, the observance of the ancient laws and the interpretation and reform of this constitution. Evidently Bentham had carefully thought out this constitution even though only this bare outline dedicated specifically to Colombia appears in his papers at University College. After each title, he placed the number of articles in each and at the end gave the total number of articles as 191.[14] Perhaps this was the tabula referred to by Bentham in a letter to Simon Bolívar in August of 1825.

Bolívar had visited James Mill at Bentham's home in 1810, and, although Bentham had seen him there, he had not deigned to meet him at that time. But when it became apparent that Bolívar

13. *Ibid.*
14. "Colombia Constitutional Code A," May 30, 1822, in UCL, XII, 64.

would determine the destiny of a large part of Spanish America, Bentham began writing to him. In the letter of August, 1825, Bentham told Bolívar that he was sending him: (1) "Principles that ought to guide in the formation of a Constitutional Code for a state," (2) "Declaration or Protest of every individual of the Legislative Body on taking possession of his office," (3) "Official aptitude maximized, expense minimized," (4) *Tabula of the contents of the Constitutional Code by the titles of chapters and section.* ("It may serve as a map that is of the field of law and legislature.") In addition Bentham was sending several copies of his *Codification Proposal* in Spanish and English. He informed Bolívar that his entire constitutional code would have been completed a year ago except that he had not finished the section on the judiciary, but, he assured Bolívar, the entire code would be finished before he had time to respond to Bentham's letter. In one of the most detailed discussions involving the problems of drawing up the code, Bentham told Bolívar that in order to draw up the procedural code he had had to predetermine the penal and civil codes. As to the penal code, many of its leading principles had been thoroughly fixed in the first four works of Bentham's that Dumont had edited in French. But the civil code would take much longer because of the mass of detail necessary.[15]

After a rather lengthy explanation of the organization of this code, Bentham launched into a strong defense of such an "all-comprehensive Code in contradistinction to the dream called *Common Law*, declared by unauthorized individuals from the decisions of judges in individual cases." He pointed to his own homeland where *codification* and *codify*, words of his own invention, were no longer objects of ridicule but were now in common usage among public functionaries. In the English Parliament there was even discussion of moving toward a comprehensive code, but this was naturally opposed by "the body of lawyers . . . a part of the useless burden of Common Law." And in the United States more and more interest was being shown in Bentham's work.[16]

15. Bentham to Simón Bolívar, August 13, 1825, in UCL XII, 235–37.
16. *Ibid.*, 340.

Then Bentham turned to Bolívar and the code. By appeals to his sense of duty as well as by patent flattery, Bentham attempted to convert Bolívar to his views, thereby achieving for himself a degree of control over the Liberator and his actions. He began by calling attention to the basic premise of his code, that is, the provision for the greatest happiness to the many, which required a sacrifice from the ruling few. He continued, "If there be, or can ever be a . . . state, in which this necessary sacrifice presents a chance of being made, it is the State, or rather those States, the destinies of which at present are, and by all lovers of mankind in this country (not to speak of others) it is most ardently hoped will, for no small length of time continue to be in your hands." Bentham told the Liberator he was confident that Bolívar, so accustomed to sacrifice, would use the weight of his authority to bring about similar sacrifice from those under him, but he warned that this would be scarcely less difficult than subduing those enemies of independence. At this point, Bentham moved on to the various reports of assassination attempts on the life of the Liberator. He assured Bolívar that once "that form of government which in profession has the greatest happiness to the greatest number for its end" was firmly established, "the political enemies of the founder of it will not behold in his destruction any prospect of advantage, capable of counterbalancing the danger and infamy of a murderous attempt." He referred to Washington, pointing out that once the constitution was established, eliminating Washington would have changed little.[17] All of this effort was to no avail, however, for in the *Cartas del Libertador* is a letter from Bolívar to Bentham dated January 15, 1827, which informed Bentham that he had not received his letter of August 13, 1825, until the end of December, 1826. Much to his displeasure, Bolívar reported that he had not received any of the items Bentham said he was sending him nor had he met Mr. Nicholas Mill who was supposedly delivering them. He apologized for his lack of reply stating simply, "the fault was not mine." Then he asked Bentham to send him again the

17. *Ibid.*, 341–43.

works of civil and judicial legislation as well as other information which he eagerly awaited.[18]

Bentham had better luck with an Englishman, Francis Hall, who had gone to Colombia with General John Devereux in 1822 serving as a colonel. Bentham maintained correspondence with Hall over a number of years, and Hall enthusiastically worked to achieve Bentham's goals for Spanish America. In 1824, Hall published a small book, *Colombia: Its Present State and Inducements to Emigration.* This descriptive essay, designed to lure British settlers to Colombian shores, was dedicated to Bentham: "I take the liberty of dedicating the following page to *you*, because I am convinced there is no one more aware of the evils of a crowded population, and defective social institutions, or who would more gladly anticipate in the New World such improved forms of political existence as we must almost despair of witnessing in the old." In regard to the code, Hall reported to Bentham, "You will be pleased to know that your ideas on legislation are gaining ground in Colombia; a law of Congress of the 11th of June, 1823, order, that all laws shall be accompanied by an *exordium,* containing the fundamental reasons for their enactment. I have no doubt that this idea was suggested by the present of your *Codification Proposal* to this government. For *its* sake, rather than *yours,* I could have wished the obligation had been acknowledged." Bentham had sent Hall a copy of his *Codification Proposal* in 1822, according to a letter dated May 17, 1822, which states, "The accompanying paper beginning *Codification Proposal* will speak for itself." Perhaps Hall had been able to give publicity to Bentham's ideas in Colombia.[19]

Bentham did not ignore the possibilities of action brought about by appeals to important groups as well as to significant individuals. In July and August of 1826 he wrote a letter to the legislators of Mexico and Colombia which may or may not have been

18. Vicente Lecuna (ed.), *Cartas del Libertador* (12 vols.; Caracas, 1929–1959), VI, 154–55.

19. Francis Hall, *Colombia: Its Present State and Inducements to Emigration* (London, 1824), preface, 5, 7; Bentham to Francis Hall, May 17, 1822, in UCL, XII, 62.

finished and dispatched. Curiously this document's single theme was something other than Bentham as codifier. Instead here, forgetting his self-promotion, he argues for giving any code adopted a temporary status, stating, "Immutability is in proportion to the goodness of a law needless: besides its mischievousness." While he informed them of his own codification work soon to be finished on the judiciary establishment, the procedure code, and the penal code and reminded them of the samples they had of his constitutional code, he described these his labors as "a feather in the scale" compared to the importance of temporariness. Indeed, "but for this temporariness, Anglo-American liberty would have been nipt in the bud." His proposal to them was simply this: "1. Of delay, not a moment, 2. Nothing but temporariness in all these Codes."[20]

Finally in 1826 Bentham's dream came true, at least partially, for he was asked for assistance in drawing up a code for a Spanish American state. But strangely Bentham virtually refused. By the time this request came, Bentham was seventy-eight years old and beginning to despair of ever finishing his codification work. He contented himself with general recommendations of another's work and the posting of parts of his own. Nevertheless, he was pleased and flattered by this invitation and began a warm correspondence with José del Valle, who asked for his aid. Del Valle began by informing Bentham that his works had given him "the glorious title of legislator of the world." Then he told Bentham that the state assembly of Guatemala had appointed him to the committee whose function it was to draw up the civil code:

I have turned eyes to you, and your worthy works. I have some: I lack others, and your thoughts would be of infinite value to me.

Permit me to ask you to turn your attention to a republic which is just born, and whose happiness is of the highest interest to me. Please send me your thoughts. Know that they will be appreciated by the one who offers to you his respect and consideration.[21]

20. Several fragmentary drafts are in Jeremy Bentham, 1826 (MMS, British Museum, Additional Manuscripts) 33551, hereinafter cited as Add. MSS.

21. José del Valle to Bentham, 1826, in UCL, XII, 346.

Bentham responded to this request with enthusiasm. On November 10, 1826, he wrote del Valle, "The accompanying packet will speak more forcible [sic] than any words in a Letter can do, my respect for your commands, and the ardency of my desire, to render my labours, such as they are, as serviceable as may be to the newfound state, from which you have received a task, in which all other tasks are comprehended." Bentham confirmed his view of the significance of the code, particularly one that is based on the greatest happiness principle when he wrote, "The place occupied by Guatemala in the American hemisphere, is the place occupied by the Sun in the system which bears his name: May it be the radiant point from which light to others is diffused!"[22]

In spite of this enthusiasm and his evident desire to help del Valle, Bentham did not provide immediate assistance. He did, however, tell del Valle that he had heard that he had a copy of Edward Livingston's draught of a penal code, which he had been told was based on the principles of Dumont's edition of Bentham's *Traités de Legislation*. While Bentham promised to send by the next ship a copy of the table of contents and titles of his penal code, he recommended that del Valle, in the meantime, might gain assistance from Livingston's work. Then with the comment, "Almost any law is better than none," he recommended, "The best thing you could do would be to give adoption, all at once, to the Code without waiting to see what, if anything, I may be able to furnish." But, Bentham added, returning once more to his theme, whatever course the state took, it should be expressly temporary without the intent of perpetuating what might be sad and inadequate as the poor Spaniards had done.[23]

Bentham sent to del Valle as much as 464 closely printed pages of his constitutional code along with 300 pages of this code which had been translated into Spanish. He promised to "apply my

22. Bentham to del Valle, November 10, 1826, in UCL, XII, 353.
23. *Ibid.*, 355. About this time a Guatemalan, José Francisco Barrundia, began the translation of the Livingston codes into Spanish and in 1837 they went into effect in the state of Guatemala. See Mario Rodríguez, *The Livingston Codes in the Guatemalan Crisis of 1837–1838* (New Orleans, 1955).

thought to the sending to you such parts of them (penal and civil codes) as capable of being detached and capable of being of use independently of the rest." Ever mindful of his age, he prefaced this remark with, "I am anxious that my papers will be in the hands of men who to the ability will add the inclination and endeavour to compleat them for your use."[24]

Del Valle reacted warmly to this interest of the "light of Westminster." In a letter dated April 18, 1827, he responded with warmth, praise, and flattery as he told Bentham that he had received his letter and books.

In my library your works will hold the distinguished station to which the sage instructor of the legislators of the world is entitled. By their influence, I trust a happy revolution will be brought about among all the nations of the earth. You have reared the science upon a fruitful principle—that of universal utility—giving lessons of addition and substraction [sic]—of legislative arithmetic—teaching the calculations of good and evil—to group—to deduct—to obtain balances of pain and pleasure—and to form law with a view to the greatest felicity. And having revolutionized the science of legislation, you will revolutionize legislative codes—so that nations will have laws—not the opprobrium, but the honor of reason—laws not the misfortune, but the happiness of man.[25]

Del Valle continued telling Bentham of his own denunciation of the existing Spanish codes and the necessity of new codes influenced "by the sages who have perfected the jurisprudential science." He then enumerated his endeavours to this end, which included writing the instructions for Guatemala's deputies to the Spanish Cortes, which stressed the necessity of a legislative code to remedy the grievances under the old Spanish one. He closed his letter in a manner that must have pleased its recipient: "To you I shall write by any safe channel. The wise are to me the most illustrious of beings. Merchants may correspond about metallic interests, but the interests of knowledge are far more important."[26]

In what was perhaps the last letter of del Valle to Bentham

24. Bentham to del Valle, November 10, 1826, in UCL, XII, 381–84.
25. Del Valle to Bentham, April 18, 1827, in Add. MSS 33546, BM.
26. Ibid.

dated August 3, 1831, del Valle, whose love of praise was probably second only to Bentham's, once more flattered Bentham with,

How I envy my cousin—with how much delight would I change my fate with his, that I might dwell in the abode of the best legislator of the world!

I shall take care to give circulation to your Constitutional Code. The light from Westminster shall illumine these lands.[27]

27. Del Valle to Bentham, August 3, 1831, in Add. MSS 33546, BM. Prospero de Herrera, a Central American agent in Europe, was guest at Queen Square Place from time to time.

Three

GOVERNMENT

BENTHAM FORESAW SPANISH AMERICA as an area destined to stability and equity, where the universal interest of the subject many would always predominate over those of the ruling few. This would come about, Bentham believed, to the degree that these Spanish American states accepted and implemented his ideas, specifically his codes. But his constitutional code was still incomplete, and these new-born nations had to be governed in some fashion—code or no code.

In his efforts to further his cause in Spanish America, Bentham encouraged the establishment of the republican form of government and warned against any attempts at a constitutional monarchy. Yet he specifically disliked the federal system and cautioned the leaders to make no permanent commitment to such an organization of power. While pleased with a republican structure, he understood its intrinsic problems, in particular how to create a literate electorate and how to control the drive for personal power. Even so Bentham was gratified by the political achievements of some Spanish American leaders, particularly Bernardino Rivadavia in Buenos Aires. Yet Bentham had information that, in spite of his own endeavors and the desires of many well-wishers, the conditions in Spanish America were hardly conducive to the growth of the Benthamic utopia of which he dreamed.

His pleasure at the republican nature of the new governments brought forth from Bentham an open admission of his own republican sympathies. In a letter to Bolívar dated August 13, 1825, Bentham twice stated this. In the fragment of the letter in the University College collection, he wrote, "But being, as I am, an avowed Republican";[1] later in a portion of the letter found in *Memorias del General O'Leary*, he repeated, "I am a republican, declared as such frankly and by the press."[2] He openly denounced the monarchical form and could see no reason why Spanish America might want it. In a letter to Rivadavia in 1820, he began, "You wish for a King for Buenos Ayres and Chili: so, at least, I understand from our friend Laurence. If so, much good may it do you. But how much better would you be with a king than the Anglo-Americans without one? The Spaniards have a reason, such as it is, for having a king. But you have not that reason—nor ever had."[3]

Bentham detested absolute monarchy yet he cared little more for the constitutional monarch. Much of his correspondence contains denunciations, even diatribes, against the English government. And the long letters to the Spanish people, "Emancipation Spanish" and *Rid Yourselves of Ultramaria*, reflect his opposition to what he termed "mixt monarchy" because it fostered the corruptive influence.

The one government that seemed to measure up to Bentham's standards was that of the Anglo-American United States, and he frequently recommended that Spanish America follow the example set by its northern neighbor. Again and again he referred to it as the best government yet devised and as one based on his greatest happiness principle. Even so, this government was not perfect. Bentham's primary objection to the United States government lay in its federal system—a system which was fast becoming a vital part of Spanish American liberals' programs. In two separate letters to del Valle, Bentham denounced the federal form. He began by stating that his constitutional code made no provision for such organization because of the difficulties involved. He pointed out that "for a model taken in the aggregate, nothing so

1. Bentham to Simón Bolívar, August 13, 1825, in UCL, XII, 340.
2. Simon B. O'Leary (ed.), *Memorias del General O'Leary* (32 vols.; Caracas, 1879–1914), XII, 275.
3. Bowring (ed.), *Works*, X, 513.

good elsewhere could assuredly have been found" than the United States. Yet even this strong nation with its vast pecuniary resources had "every now and then been in as much danger of depression, accompanied perhaps with civil war, so great is the difficulty of securing punctual and truly proportioned contributions from each particular state to the central government." Taxes then formed the major obstacle to the successful operation of the federal system and, while the United States suffered inconvenience, "that inconvenience seems likely to be to an indefinite degree augmented in the case of yours." The federal form required as well a dual judiciary system, with the inherent difficulty of drawing lines between the two jurisdictions and the increased expense of the two separate courts. In addition, the federal pattern ran the risk, intentional or not, of taxes or bounties applied to one article for one purpose hurting or reducing "the profit upon production, importation or exportation of this or that article to which it is applied for the other purpose."[4]

Bentham's solution for this problem in Spanish America was what he termed a simpler one. While states might exist, there would be a single judiciary. Each of the states would be required to pay a quota of money to the central treasury before the state could use any money for itself. This system would be based on universal registration and universal publication so that no receipt or expenditure could be made in one state without the central government and every other state knowing of it "as soon as the post can convey it." The enormous task of registration and publication would be achieved by one of Bentham's pet schemes, the manifold mode. It seems that Bentham was content to allow the federal system to operate along certain lines if the financial and judical arrangements could be clarified. Even so, Bentham urged, "But whatever you do in this way, you should by all means forbear any such attempt as that of giving perpetuity to it."[5]

Bentham believed that the electorate, to a great degree, determined the success of any representative government, federal or

4. Bentham to del Valle, 1826–1827, in UCL, XII, 360, 384, 360, 361.
5. *Ibid.*, 362, 384.

otherwise. Quite early Bentham had sketched out some ideas about voting in Spanish America. In the document entitled "Intended for Caracas on the Occasion of General Miranda's Expedition," Bentham suggested as item number two that persons not be allowed to vote until they have reached a certain age, "say 20," and have the ability to read and write, the latter being proven by his signature on the spot. This section, however, has a single mark through the center as though he might have meant it to be deleted. However, on page 76 of this document he turned again to the literacy qualifications for voting. Bentham here recommended that proof of ability to write be given by copying in the voter's own handwriting the laws relative to voting. The right to vote should require as well the capability of forming a rational judgment which comes by being able to read. Those who could not read and write would be excluded from voting until they learned. Thus voting would be a reward for this achievement which is "the most efficient instrument of general civilization." But how could this nation just a-borning finance extensive literacy instruction? Bentham recommended the Lancaster method, (see Chapter Seven) which would cost a "mere trifle."[6]

Understanding the frailty of the recently created representative institutions, Bentham was particularly apprehensive about a possible drive for personal power by the Spanish American liberators and their assistants. He watched for evidence of such action and occasionally took up his pen to give warning to those he feared were moving in the wrong direction. One of the first instances of this is found in a letter to Rivadavia dated October 3, 1818. "Another object that extends the face without calming it," Bentham wrote, "is your Supreme Director; through this Supremacy of whose duration I see no limit, he believes to see eternity." He continued by lashing out at the decrees issued by Juan Martín de Pueyrredón with the approval of the congress, asking why Congress itself did not issue the decree that, "listening to the Supreme Director with his decree, it would say he alone thinks and orders."

6. "Intended for Caracas on the Occasion of General Miranda's Expedition," 1810, in UCL, XXI, 57, 56.

Then he attacked Rivadavia for failing to take appropriate action to achieve utilitarian goals: "Is it that the Republic with its liberty does not exist except in hope? And you, yourself, Señor, have you not let go for the next year the realization of the ideas that so much please us both? You see here our doubts, but they are the doubts of a friend, of a respectful friend that remains one."[7]

As Simón Bolívar gained ascendancy in northern South America, Bentham became increasingly interested in him, his government, and the possibilities of influencing his decisions. Found in his papers at University College, London, is an extract from José Turbicio Echeverría's "Dos Palabras," which had been translated by Sarah Taylor Austin. Echeverría, an agent for Bolívar's government in London, had penned a lengthy description of the struggle for independence in Spanish America which turned into a panegyric for Bolívar.

Bolivar, who cannot be ignorant that he is the sole director of the armed force and the idol of the people? Will he seek to be the Washington or the Buonaparte [sic] of Colombia? Oh wonder! Bolivar was infinitely more a hero in the halls of Congress than he had ever been in the field of battle . . . not only did he then swear to obey that law which leveled his rights with those of the most wretched labourers; not only did he spontaneously denounce the just influence which his virtues and his exploits exercise over the spirit of his countrymen . . . so incredible a height arose his love of liberty and his noble frankness, that he denounced himself as dangerous to the new born freedom of the country, in order that he might be deprived of the means of ever working its mischief.[8]

Such enthusiasm for Bolívar was probably shared to some degree by Bentham. On December 24, 1820, he wrote Bolívar telling him of his letter to Spain demanding the independence of Spanish America "whatever slice of their Ultramaria you may happen to take a fancy to, unless I see reason for thinking that there would be better hands for it, which does not seem likely, let me know what it is,—I will do what depends upon me towards *your* having it." Bentham wanted to be sure, however, that he was absolutely

7. Bentham to Rivadavia, October 3, 1818, in Add. MSS 33545–6, BM.
8. José Turbicio Echeverría, "Dos Palabras," translated by Sarah Taylor Austin, undated, in UCL XII, 58–60.

understood: "Always understand *you* in the plural number, and not in the *singular.*" Then, for emphasis, he added, "I have a notion of viz. that if it be not your design to form to yourself a monarch transmissible to natural descendants, you would, during your lifetime, with little more nominal power than the President of the Anglo-American United States, have as much effective power as if you were acknowledged absolute and exercise it, in a manner much more pleasant to all parties."[9]

In an undated fragmentary letter, Bentham told Bolívar, with a degree of respect, that he had read in the *Morning Chronicle* of December 26, 1818, of his proposal to call a representative assembly (Cucuta). He followed this, however, by quoting a report from an English gentleman in whom he had perfect confidence who had told him of Bolívar's "putting to death with your own hands a large number of Spaniards them being at your disposal in the quality of prisoners." Bentham continued, "I can have no appearance of supporting it." Then he agreed Bolívar must suffer many provocations, and while he did not condemn Bolívar, he made it clear to the Liberator that the world was watching him.[10]

José de San Martín did not fare nearly so well with Bentham. In the single letter addressed to San Martín found at University College in what is probably Bentham's own hand, he lectured and severely criticized San Martín on his role as Protector of Peru. "Let the direction be temporary and the end in view and real design a republican democracy as soon as the state of the country is ripe for it, not only the end, but eventually the very means." Bentham, unaware at this early day of the manner in which Spanish America would institutionalize the dictator, thought that this office could serve in a benign way to create the proper atmosphere for an effective republican government. Accordingly, if *protector* meant *dictator* and nothing more, then Bentham expected San Martín to look with favour on the proposals for codification that Bentham was sending him; if, however, *protector* meant *emperor* the reaction would be unfavorable. Bentham informed San Martín that if he

9. Bentham to Bolívar, December 24, 1820, in UCL, CLXIII, 26–7.
10. Bentham to Bolívar, undated, in UCL, X, 5–6.

would be dictator only, then San Martín would search for useful and appropriate information for his people and would speak more often of the people's rights than their duties and more of his own duties and less of his rights. Bentham told San Martín that he was sending a duplicate of this letter to Bolívar. Then to add insult to injury, Bentham told San Martín that while confidence grew slowly, everything he knew of Bolívar made its growth accelerate, while what he knew of San Martín made him pause. Strangely enough, following this disparagement, Bentham listed testimonials for his various works. But soon he returned to this theme. If as protector San Martín meant to establish order and then step aside for republican development, fine. But, "if on the other hand he be in design a Caesar, may that Caesar if nothing else will suffice find a Brutus, is the undissembled wish of Jeremy Bentham."[11]

Perhaps Bentham was quite serious about this, or perhaps he was simply taken by the turn of phrase. On June 13, 1822, in a letter to San Martín's fellow Argentine Rivadavia, Bentham congratulated Rivadavia upon his trade policy, then commented, "It forms a striking contrast with the course which I have the mortification to see taken by two infant states your juniors, viz. Peru under the self styled Protector, and Mexico, under we know not as yet whom or what." He told Rivadavia of his correspondence with San Martín "as yet only on one side nor do I see any near prospect of its having place on both sides." Bentham continued in the same tone as the one in his San Martín letter: "If Protector means nothing more than *Dictator*, and to no other end than that of setting up a good Representative Democracy, it is the very thing I had on a certain supposition, been wishing for: if instead of Dictator, Caesar, then my wish is—that if nothing else will serve Caesar may find his Brutus." Bentham concluded his comments on San Martín to Rivadavia by saying that while expectations of the Protector were still favorable, he believed having a Caesar as neighbor would be disagreeable to him.[12]

11. Bentham to José de San Martín, May 31–June 6, 1822, in UCL, XII, 65–74.
12. Bentham to Rivadavia, June 13, 1822, in UCL, XII, 387–88. This document is a partial copy (complete except for the last half of the fourth page) in a clearer

At the bottom of a page which looks as though it was to be the last page of the letter to San Martín, headed by the instruction "to be transcribed on another sheet," Bentham came as near an apology as he ever did: "Believe me, Sir, it grieves me to the heart to think of the liberties I have felt obliged to take with you. I would cast myself at your feet if by any such gesture I had an assurance that there my endeavours would be facilitated. Though you can scarcely have a less agreeable one anywhere, you can not have a more sincere friend in any one than in me." This is a brief paragraph, however, for the next sheet begins "mortification upon mortification" followed by a description of Bentham's horror upon reading in the *Morning Chronicle* of that day about San Martín's creation of the Order of the Sun. "Sir, the character and effect of it is (I hope) altogether unknown to you. Real merit demonstrated by real service" is not rewarded in such fashion. For that matter "even for military merit, this is not the most apt honorary reward." Bentham suggested to San Martín, "Think, sir, of the once projected Order of Cincinnaticus if it be that you ever heard of it. In its origin, in its nature, it was to a prodigious degree less bad than this Order of the Sun." Bentham lambasted such orders as indicative of "everything that is most base in the human character." Real service to universal interest prohibited such orders and such orders allowed and perhaps encouraged corruption, which to Bentham was the greatest evil.[13] No evidence exists in the Bentham manuscripts at University College Library or the British Museum as to the result of this letter—or if it was even posted.

Bentham continued in any case to follow the actions taken by the new governments as carefully as he could, hoping that they would adhere to his designs and wishes. From time to time proof came of Spanish America's adherence to utilitarian principles. In

---

amanuensis' hand, of Bentham's letter of June 13 and 15, 1822, headed "J. B. to Bernardino Rivadavia Secretary of State in Buenos Ayres," UCL, LX, 16–19. A. Taylor Milne (ed.), *Catalogue of the Manuscripts of Jeremy Bentham in the Library of University College, London* (London, 1962), inaccurately lists the document XII, 387–88 as a letter to José del Valle.

13. Bentham to San Martín, May 31–June 6, 1822, in UCL, XII, 75–80. The date of the *Morning Chronicle* is June 4, 1822.

August of 1822 Rivadavia sent Bentham the rule he had drawn up for the Buenos Aires legislative assembly. He told his English friend that it was "entirely based on your unimpeachable and indisputable truths contained in your work on the *Táctica* of Legislative Assemblies."[14] Bentham did not receive this letter until April 5, 1824. He thanked Rivadavia for it but made little further comment.[15] However, Bentham was evidently pleased at this act of his disciple because in September of that same year he sent Rivadavia's rule to the legislative assembly of Greece with a warm commendation of Rivadavia as the founder of Buenos Aires and his state as the only state in Spanish and Portuguese America "which has taken a firm and happy footing." Rivadavia's letter in its original French with an English translation, together with the letter to Greece, became parts of the Testimonials section of Bentham's *Codification Proposal*. Bentham appreciated this evidence of his influence but seemingly only because it proved his position in Rivadavia's thinking. He was not the least interested in its substance, apparently feeling that he knew without study the design of Rivadavia's rule. At any rate, in the letter to Greece and in a letter to del Valle on November 10, 1826, Bentham openly admitted that he had never found time to read Rivadavia's work.[16]

In the same letter, Rivadavia listed other plans which also proved his adherence to Bentham's philosophy. These included a national bank on a solid financial base, reform of the bureaucracy and the military allowing for fair salary and the end of their useless increase in numbers, protection of individual security, initiation of public works of recognized utility, protection of commerce and the sciences and arts, reduction of customs, and ecclesiastical reform. All in all, these were changes, as Rivadavia quite aptly put it, that would win Bentham's approval. And, with this approval, Rivadavia believed that he would have the necessary strength to execute such a program.[17]

14. Rivadavia to Bentham, August 26, 1822, in Add. MSS 33545, BM.

15. Bentham to Rivadavia, April 5, 1824, in UCL, XII, 269–74.

16. Bowring (ed.), *Works*, IV, 584–85, 592–93; Bentham to del Valle, November 10, 1826, in UCL, XII, 356.

17. Rivadavia to Bentham, August 26, 1822, in Add. MSS 33545, BM.

Rivadavia received praise from Bentham for his economic policy as well. "What more particularly struck me is—the magnanimity and true sense of national as well as universal interest displayed by the putting as far as depends upon laws and treaties, all nations upon the same footing in respect of commerce." Bentham continued by regretting what Peru and Mexico had done and wondering what Bolívar would do, "and on this head [Bolívar's] there can be no better hope than that of seeing it follow your example."[18]

Bentham probably felt that Rivadavia was moving toward achievement of his, Bentham's, highest dreams for Spanish America. He proudly kept in his papers transcribed copies of some of the orders given by Rivadavia that came into his possession. In addition to these he also had copied from the *Morning Chronicle* items of interest about the governments of Buenos Aires, Peru, and Chile. Two of the ordinances transcribed from the paper pertained to a Buenos Aires order dealing with drunkenness and the prohibition of a game called *Pato*. The Peruvian section included news of a new flag and the government's invitation for bids for the building of two stone bridges. Information about Chile told of the call for the election of representatives from each Chilean municipality to a constitutional convention called by Bernardo O'Higgins to meet July 1, 1822, for three months. One piece of collectanea in the University College Library collection is from the *Traveller*, November 29, 1821, which gives the "Fundamental Law of the Union of the People of Colombia" uniting Venezuela and New Granada into one republic, Colombia.[19]

Bentham got a quite candid view of Spanish American political development from his other major Spanish American source, Englishmen living abroad, specifically Colonel Francis Hall. Hall, in a letter from Bogotá written in October of 1822, bluntly informed Bentham that "the mass of the people is ignorant, timid, and su-

18. Bentham to Rivadavia, June 13 and 15, 1822, in UCL, XII, 387.
19. Executive orders of Rivadavia, in UCL, LX, 44–45; item from *Traveller*, November 29, 1821, in UCL, XXI 24; items from *Morning Chronicle*, 1821–1822, in UCL, CIX, 210.

perstitious, and their chiefs too rarely form exceptions to the general rule." Bentham had earlier suggested in a letter that Hall might try to get Colombia to institute his Panoptican plan for prisons and then Hall could be its administrator. Hall's response is about as tart and frank on the circumstances in Spanish America as any found in letters to Bentham:

You will scarcely expect, my dear Sir, that with its hands as full as they are at present, the Govt should be *well* disposed to turn much of its attention towards your excellent plans of prison reform. In fact they have much to reform ere they come to the Prison—Schools, Churches, Courts of Justice. The Senate, itself, will need the same salutary medicine, which, I am sorry to say, is for some time likely to be slowly and partially administered. A few Enlightened men are to be met with, rare . . . but the Philanthropist or Philosopher will derive little satisfaction from a general contemplation of the national character—he may apologize for its defects, but he must acknowledge them to be numerous—God knows how they have got on so far as they have.[20]

This, then, from the man who was to urge Englishmen to immigrate to Colombia! But this was mild compared to Hall's evaluation of the political situation in a letter to William Empson, editor of the *Edinburgh Review*, a transcribed copy of which Bentham made when Empson allowed him to read the letter.

There is besides a spirit of hostility towards the present system of Govt growing up even in the minds of the firmest patriots and best wishers to Independence . . . the cause of all this is easily unfolded. During all the changes of the Revolution, the mass of the people, has seen little change, but a change of masters. The Constitution however fallacious in its general structure still presents some *points d'appri* to liberty, but the Constitution has been always used like a child's bauble, shewn to him on holidays and then laid aside lest he should break it. Under the denomination of 'Provinces which are the seat of war' or 'are adjacent to those which are the seat of war' or 'such as are likely to become the seat of war'—the whole country has been subjected to a military despotism, in the hands of the Executive and his Delegates, the local military authorities. All this is

20. Francis Hall to Bentham, October 17, 1822, in UCL, XII, 85.

the necessary consequence of the central system, in a country so vast, un-passable and depopulated, but the central system has been upheld for the sake of this consequence and has now to fight it out with Federalism. If it succeeds, you will probably hear of some *royal* doings which will effec-tually stifle the infant Liberty in the cradle. Sorry ambition which aspires only to be on a level with the beloved Ferdinand and the two gouty flesh mountains George and Louis.[21]

Evidently Bentham became concerned by the starkness of Hall's descriptions of Colombia. Another copy of an Empson letter from Hall in the Bentham collection bears the heading in Ben-tham's hand "seen but not published. J. B." In this letter, Hall told Empson that Colombia was headed toward despotism, "more per-haps from ignorance and bad habit than design." The legislature was reduced to a rubber stamp because everyone had extraordi-nary powers. Thus people even rightly motivated never seemed to do what was right and rational. Illustrative of this was the crea-tion of the High Police, "worse than ten Inquisitions." In a later letter to Empson, Hall described the difficulties facing Colombia: "It can not however be denied that Colombia finds herself at pres-ent in the condition of a person, who, with a feeble constitution, has made a violent effort, overstrained, out of joint, nerveless and powerless." He continued by commenting that Bolívar was in Peru where he was said to have lost two battles. "Peru ought to be ade-quate to her own deliverance, if not, Colombia will hardly prop her."[22]

But Bentham may not have taken such views at face value. Per-haps he knew that Hall had aligned himself with a particular po-litical group which could color his judgment. In any case the Ben-tham manuscripts contain a transcribed copy of an article in the *Morning Chronicle* of April 19, 1822, of a portion of a letter from Caracas dated January, 1822, which tends to put Hall's statements in a little different perspective. It reads, "The character of these people is very little understood in England. It has chiefly reached

21. *Ibid.*, 108.
22. *Ibid.*, 135, 136.

the British public through the representations of disappointed officers, who liking neither fighting nor hard fare, returned to home to write books containing representations which they knew there was nobody in England to contradict."[23]

23. Item from *Morning Chronicle*, April 19, 1822, in UCL, CIX, 238.

Four

"EMANCIPATION SPANISH"

BENTHAM KNEW THAT INDEPENDENCE FROM SPAIN was a prerequisite for the creation in Spanish America of his utilitarian states, and he argued long and hard for such independence. But in actuality Bentham's desire to see the end of empire antedates his interest in Spanish America by decades. In a series of essays on the "Principles of International Law" written between 1786 and 1789, Bentham listed the emancipation of colonies as one of the six requisites for lasting peace among nations.[1] It is not strange then that once he becomes interested in Spanish America his longest Spanish American documents are attempts to persuade the Spaniards to free their New World empire. As he pled the cause of Spanish American independence, Bentham delineated his views of empire and used the opportunity for an incisive critique of the Spanish Constitution of 1812.

Spain had been of interest to Bentham for a long time, for his works were well known there through the translations of Pierre Etienne Dumont. It became a particular focal point, however, as the possibilities of governmental change there became apparent. As a direct outgrowth of Napoleon's move into Spain, the Spanish people began to consider fundamental changes in their political system. Bentham followed subsequent events in Spain particularly through correspondence with Blanco White, the editor of *El Español*. In a letter to Bentham on October 24, 1810, White wrote,

1. Bowring (ed.), *Works*, II, 546.

"your works . . . will have a material influence in the future code of Spanish laws, if we ever come to possess such a blessing."[2]

It was much later, in 1820, shortly after he learned of the New Year's day pronouncement of Colonel Rafael Riego and his allies demanding a return to the Constitution of 1812 that Bentham began his long letters to the Spanish people arguing for the emancipation of Spanish colonies. Even though he was aware that many parts of the Spanish empire were virtually independent by this time, he used the Revolution of 1820 as justification for writing many pages on the subject of empire. Why he chose to do so is not clear. Perhaps he was interested in ending the armed conflicts; perhaps he was concerned with the legality of the revolutions, or perhaps it was simply his belief that empires were inherently detrimental to liberal governments.

These manuscripts were not, however, the first detailed statement of Bentham's attitude toward colonies, for in 1792 he had written *Emancipate Your Colonies, addressed to the National Convention of France, 1793; Showing the uselessness and mischievousness of Distant Dependencies to a European State.* He had had it printed privately and distributed copies of it among his friends. In his messages to Spain he consistently referred to it and promised to attach a copy for study. In addition, in 1818, he had written "Emancipation Preface," which contains in outline form many of the ideas about empire he was to develop later.[3]

While the 1793 *Emancipate Your Colonies* emphasized the economic value of independence, the letters of 1820–1822 to the Spanish people dealt in much more depth and detail with the problems of empire. The first 1820 manuscript begun on April 30, 1820, was entitled "Spaniards Emancipate Your Colonies by Philo Hispanus." Some time thereafter Bentham began a work which on February 8, 1822, he entitled "Rid Yourselves of Ultramaria: Being the advice of Jeremy Bentham as given in a series of Letters to the Spanish people."[4] These two documents differ little in content and

2. *Ibid.*, X, 456.
3. *Ibid.*, IV, 407–18; "Emancipation Preface," 1818, in UCL, VIII, 1–9.
4. "Emancipation Preface," 1818, in UCL, VIII, 11, 64.

they seem to merge into a statement of Bentham's ideas concerning the Spanish colonies. The earlier document "Emancipation Spanish," in which Bentham referred to Spanish America as Creolia, drew rather heavily for substantiating data on Joseph Townsend's *A Journey through Spain in the Years 1786 and 1787.* The later document, "Rid Yourselves of Ultramaria," used a name that Bentham evidently derived from the Spanish word *Ultramar,* which was used in the Spanish Constitution in reference to overseas possessions. In the choice of titles for these letters Bentham revealed much of his reasoning. The first, "Emancipation Spanish," described his goal of liberation for the colonies, whereas the later, "Rid Yourselves," implied that Spain would be freeing herself of responsibilities and expenses.

Bentham's advice to the Spanish people in the more than thirteen hundred manuscript pages he devoted to the task fell into three broad divisions: why Spain should emancipate, the effects on Spain of emancipation, and the means of relinquishing control.

The new-found freedom under the constitution for which Bentham again and again reassuringly stated his admiration acted as a fulcrum for Bentham's arguments for liberation. The constitution, Bentham reasoned, demanded emancipation. The old government had "kept all hands in shackles . . . kept a gag in every mouth, a bandage over all eyes," but the new government under the constitution eliminated all of these, replacing them with liberty of the press and the right of memorial to the Cortes and king for all citizens. While Ultramarians had submitted to oppression before the revolution, they now shared in the new government and would no longer suffer tyranny. The idea of paradox permeated Bentham's letters: "You are but just emerged out of a tyranny and already you call your kinsmen on the other side of the Atlantic/ upon a people more numerous than yourselves to submit to yourself." And, "Ah, my friends!—this sad inconsistency—how long will it be yours? To cry out against tyranny, and all the while to concur in the exercise of it."[5]

5. "Rid yourselves of ultramaria," 1820–22, in UCL, CLXVII, 123; "Rid Yourselves of Ultramaria, being the advice of Jeremy Bentham, as given in a series of letters to the Spanish people," 1821, 1822, in UCL, VIII, 122.

Even though the new Spanish government had thrown out old restrictions, opened ports to foreigners, and allowed for liberty of the press and memorials of all citizens to the king and Cortes, still the Spanish American felt aggrieved not only by taxes but by the very existence of Spanish domination. "With such real, such ample, such universally applying cause of discontent, pervading the whole of Spanish America,—with such cause of discontent, and at the same time such unprecedented and uncontrollable means of expressing and propagating it, think whether it would be long, ere, through the several stages of disaffection and disobedience, the discontent would have ripened into revolt." This in turn would mean expensive preparations on the part of Spain to prevent the revolt's success. What then happens to the liberal thought of the constitution? Continued control of Ultramaria meant the "sacrifice of every substantial interest to the fantastic interest" called national pride.[6]

Bentham warned Spain that under the new constitution Ultramarian submission became impossible. He listed ten reasons why he thought the colonies would feel repugnance toward continued union with Spain:

1. The liberal quality of the Constitution
2. All revenue went to Spain
3. Appeals were unendurably long
4. Redress of grievances virtually impossible to attain
5. The colonies were always involved in Spanish wars
6. No Ultramarian legislatures existed
7. Representation in the Spanish Cortes provided no security against despotism
8. Ultramarian deputies were not truly representatives
9. Ultramarian rulers were ignored by Spain
10. The Constitution could not be amended for eight years.[7]

Even though Bentham consistently attacked the imperfections of the constitution, he assiduously reassured the Spanish people of his faith in it—particularly if it could be changed along the lines he recommended. The Spanish Constitution, he declared, was "a

6. "Rid yourselves of ultramaria," 1820–22, in UCL, CLXVII, 124.
7. *Ibid.*, 48–50.

compound/mixt mass of sugar and arsenic. Will you clear it of the arsenic? to a foreign hand you must be indebted for the clearance." The task faced by the codifiers, Bentham averred, was physically impossible. Assuming that the Spanish government prided itself on its utilitarian basis, Bentham pointed out that colonies by their very nature were antithetical to utilitarian principles. He argued, "As soon could the moon and earth be compressed under one government, as the greatest happiness of the greatest number in both or either be effected by a government comprizing Spain and her Ultramaria." Bentham, while commending the constitution itself, thought that the quality found there had nothing to do with Spain's rule over other areas. After all, Portugal was accepting the Spanish Constitution, but Spain had not suggested that Portugal accept Spain's rule. Why then expect Ultramaria to accept Spanish rule just because of the constitution? Bentham fundamentally indicted the Spanish Constitution then for its impossible attempt to rule both Spain and Ultramaria equally and according to the enlightened, liberal principles it professed. In his opinion, Ultramarians with equal rights and privileges would not allow Spain to continue dominion over them. Thus, to Bentham, the very enlightened, liberal quality of the constitution meant that Spain and her colonies could not be kept under the same government.[8]

Bentham's knowledge of the activities of the Cortes and the role of the Spanish American representatives in that body was sorely limited. Yet this did not deter Bentham. He had a copy of the constitution and his own ideas on empire. These were all he needed to give lengthy advice and warning to Spain. Bentham felt keenly about the constitution. He had followed its creation carefully, and its stated purpose followed the basic utilitarian maxim, the greatest happiness to the greatest number, which brought him extreme pride and joy.[9] Bentham declared that under the old government

8. *Ibid.*, 96, 256, 130, 49.
9. "Art. 13—El objeto del Gobierno es la felicidad de la Nación puesto que el fin de toda sociedad política no es otro que el bienestar de los individuos que la componen," from "Constitución Política de la Monarquía Española promulgada en Cádiz el 19 Marzo de 1812," in A. Padilla Serra (ed.), *Constituciones y Leyes Fundamentales de España, 1808–1947* (Granada, 1954), 11.

the object was the happiness of one man; under the new, the happiness of the nation, to the greatest number in the nation. Yet Spanish America already or soon would outnumber peninsular Spain; in whose interest would the Spanish government then function? How then could the constitution become anything but a dead letter if Spain insisted on maintaining its empire, this in spite of the constitution?[10]

Bentham prided himself on being able to create codes and laws for Spanish America without having any valid firsthand knowledge, but he bitterly attacked the Spanish for the same deficiency! The fatal weakness of the constitution, Bentham claimed, was the codifiers' absolute lack of knowledge of Spanish America. "No conception can the Codifiers have had from particular experience, no conception do they seem to have been able to form to themselves from imagination guided by general experience: and with all the aid they had from their self-appointed colleagues, the sham deputies from Ultramaria, any much clearer conception do they appear to have formed of themselves of the state of things in Ultramaria, in its thus projected condition, than if, instead of Ultramaria they had had the moon to deal with." Thus the only course open to Spain, Bentham believed, was emancipation. Any attempt to provide the colonies representation would not be genuine at such a distance. "Under freedom" Bentham declared, "union is not possible: only by despotism could elements, so discordant, be kept together. Slaves, you may keep your kinsmen, slaves: free, you must see them free."[11]

Bentham congratulated the Spanish for Article 373, which allowed each Spaniard to petition the king or Cortes to demand the observance of the constitution.[12] In spite of what many thought or hoped, however, Bentham saw no improvement or redress for Ultramaria under the constitution. When a Creolian functionary acted improperly and the local authorities could not remedy the

10. "Rid yourselves," 1820–22, in UCL, CLXVII, 124.
11. *Ibid.*, 115; "Emancipation Spanish," 1820, in UCL, VIII, 41, 48.
12. "Art. 373—Todo español tiene derecho de representar a las Cortes o al Rey para reclamar la observenía de la Constitución," from Serra (ed.), *Constituciones y Leyes*, 57.

situation, reference of the problem to Spain meant a lapse of a minimum of nine months from the initiation of the complaint until the decision on the case arrived back in the provinces. However, if the Cortes had to take action the delay might be much longer because the Cortes, so distant from such a disorder, had so little time to transact a mass of business. During this interim the accused would have ample time to contemplate and arrange for means to frustrate the remedy whenever it arrived. Bentham chided Spain for not establishing in its colonies some sort of legislative assembly. While the British example in India was not a pleasant one to contemplate, "that of your American kinsmen would be worse." Except in the penal colonies, Bentham continued, Britain acknowledged some legislative authority in all its colonies. Not so the Spanish, not even under the liberal constitution of 1812.[13]

The question of redress of grievances and the lack of local legislative bodies was closely tied, according to Bentham, to the constitution's prohibition against amendments for eight years after the constitution had gone into effect.[14] Here Bentham returns to his attack on the dangers of perpetuity. The provision prompted Bentham to comment:

How a set of men capable of framing a Constitution which has so much good in it could have agreed thus to insert a clause in which an assertion of infallibility is involved, seems, upon the face of the thing itself, altogether wonderful. But power has everywhere been thus short-sighted and impatient of control. . . .

The truth is every attempt on the part of the sovereignty of today to make void the acts of the sovereignty of tomorrow is itself in its own nature, void: the posterior, which should regard its hands as tied up by any such attempt of the prior authority would be as perfect a slave to superstition or the man who, by the words and grimaces of the magician,

---

13. "J.B. to Spain: Emancipate your colonies," 1820, in UCL, VIII, 34, 85; "Rid yourselves," 1820–22, in UCL, CLXVII, 119–22.

14. "Art. 375—Hasta pasado ocho años despues de hallarse puesta en práctica la Constitución en todas sus partes, no se podrá proponer alteración, adición ni reforma en ninguno de sus artículos," from Serra (ed.), *Constituciones y Leyes*, 57.

should regard himself as precluded from stepping out of the circle which the imposter has been marking out.[15]

Bentham argued forcefully that "in 2,000 years the Constitution would not have been 'carried into effect in all its parts'" so when would the eight years end? He soothed the Spanish, however, by remarking that they were simply acting as others did in this: "Not Spanish but human nature in this folly." The reason for this eight-year moratorium on change, Bentham decided, was to prevent the reestablishment of despotism. Yet if the majority wanted reestablishment of despotism, it would occur notwithstanding the prohibition of amendment for eight years. Bentham complimented the Spaniards on their constitution, calling it an object "even of *admiration* as a work of genius." Yet it had two major defects, keeping Ultramaria under Spanish control and tying posterity's hands. It was to be hoped that his lengthy letters to the Spanish people would open their eyes to these errors and bring about change.[16]

Bentham did not miss the opportunity to point out other erroneous aspects of Spain's fundamental law. Perhaps aware of Spanish America's disillusionment, he paid particular attention in the resulting analysis of the constitution to the Cortes and its powers. The Spanish were evidently pleased with the inclusion of representatives from Ultramaria in the Cortes, but Bentham determined to convince them that this was of no real value to the people in the overseas provinces. He argued that rather than a security against misrule, Creolian representation in the Cortes was an instrument of misrule because members who had "correct and prompt information" would be outvoted by those who did not. The only solution here would be to "bring the hemispheres into contact." Bentham chided the Spaniards for allowing Creoles resident in Spain to choose the Creolian representatives for the present Cortes. While this "impostrous mode" was only temporary, Bentham predicted that regularly elected Creolian members would be

15. "Rid yourselves," 1820–22, in UCL, CLXVII, 163.
16. "Rid Yourselves," 1820, in UCL, VIII, 79, 78. See also 126–27.

subject to the corruptive influence of the Spanish rulers. "The Creole representation will be filled by place hunters flocking from Creolia to Madrid, by a secret committee of Members of Legislative and Executive: as in England, so in Spain, all share. The Spanish part of the Constitution would be poisoned by the Creolian."[17]

In any case, Bentham claimed that "a full, fair and free representative of the population of Ultramaria, representative by deputies actually sent from all the several Provinces in pursuance of a full, fair and free election was utterly and manifestly impossible. . . . As an arrangement in which any claim to dominion can justly be grounded it will no more be received than a stone for bread or a serpent for fish."[18] To compensate for the dominion of Spain, Spaniards pointed out that Ultramaria had the "benefit beyond all price": the constitution and the Spanish system of representation in the Cortes. "Illusion. All illusion!" Bentham argued. Ultramaria did not have the same system of representation and could not. But even if they did, why should they submit to Spain when "they might give it to themselves taking all the benefits of it, without any of these evils."[19] Turning from Ultramaria to Spain, Bentham argued that by the share in the Cortes given to the provinces, the Spanish people themselves were done real injury because it violated the fundamental principle of the constitution: "That of not being taxed or in other respects legislated upon but by (agents) representatives chosen by yourselves." And could Ultramarian deputies know enough about Spain and its needs to have dominion through their seats in the Cortes over the Spanish people?[20]

Bentham dealt at length with the basic problem of the Ultramarian representation to the Cortes. How was it to be deter-

17. "J. B. to Spain: Emancipate your colonies," 1820, in UCL, VIII, 22. These ideas are more fully developed in "Rid yourselves," 1820–22, UCL, CLXVII, 132–35. Nettie L. Benson (ed.), *Mexico and the Spanish Cortes, 1810–1822* (Austin, Texas, 1966), illustrates the ignorance of Bentham regarding the role of Spanish Americans in the Cortes.
18. "Rid yourselves," 1820–21, in UCL, CLXVII, 225–26.
19. *Ibid.*, 126.
20. *Ibid.*, 62, 224.

mined? Bentham referred to Article 30, which based the number of deputies on a census of the Ultramarian population.[21] Until such a new census could be made, the most authentic of those latest ones would be used. But Bentham, unaware of or choosing to consider existing censuses invalid, argued that no census had ever been made. "Neither in the words of Baron Humboldt, nor in any other account of any of the Ultramarian Provinces, have I found any mention made of any *best* census. . . . What I should not be surprised to find is—that of those Ultramarian Provinces there is not so much as one in which any such census is at present in existence: what I should be much surprised if I did not find is—that in some one or more of them no such census is in existence." Furthermore, Bentham explained, no census could be actually begun until the submission of Ultramaria to Spanish control had been achieved and no census could be made because the only authority capable of ordering a census was the Provincial Deputation, which could not come into existence without the previous existence of district electors of the deputies of the Cortes. "Here, are a set of fathers who can not come into existence till after their offspring have come into the world to give it to them."[22]

Bentham continued his ridicule of the constitution's ambiguities. For each 70,000 of its population a province received one seat in the Cortes. Did this mean 70,000 males only or 70,000 males and females? If only males, then "we are compelled to understand that in the conception of the proposers and adopters of this article, such animals of the human species as are of the female sex have

21. "Art. 30—Para el cómputo de la población de los dominios europeos servirá el ultimo censo del año de mil setecientos noventa y siete, hasta que pueda hacerse otro nuevo; y se formará el correspondiente para el cómputo de la población de los de ultramar, sirviendo entre tanto los de ultramar, sirviendo entre tanto los censos más autenticos entre los ultimanente formados," from Serra (ed.), *Constituciones y Leyes*, 14.

22. "Rid yourselves," 1820–22, in UCL, CLXVII, 180, 287; "Art. 328—La elección de estos individuos (Diputaciones provinciales) se hará por los electores de partido al otro día de haber nombrado los Diputados de Cortes, por el mismo orden conque éstos se nombrian," from Serra (ed.), *Constituciones y Leyes*, 51; "J. B. to Spain: Emancipate your colonies," 1820, in UCL, VIII, 29; "Rid yourselves," 1820–22, in UCL, CLXVII, 186.

no souls." If this were not their intention, why did they use "almas" and not "hombres."[23]

In each province, it is supposed that somebody, no intimation is given who, seated (placed) on some eminence from which the whole population of the province, called before him for that purpose, are stationed within his view, begins with dividing them into groups of 70,000 human beings of both sexes taken together, or of 70,000 human beings of the male sex, with the portion of females appertaining to them and says to them, you shall constitute the population of one district.[24]

Then using a compass he would divide the land into districts naming them A, B, *etc.* "This sort of arrangement, how commodious soever, being unfortunately not a possible one, what other arrangement is there that the Code prescribes or admitts of? None such, I must acknowledge, have I been able to find."[25] By such attacks on the provision for making the constitution work in Ultramaria, Bentham hoped to demolish Spain's illusion that representation in the Cortes would effectively allay Ultramarian fears and end her grievances.

The constitution, Bentham argued, so limited the meeting time of the Cortes that, whatever its make-up, it would not have sufficient time to care for the affairs of both Spain and Ultramaria. Article 106 stated that the Cortes would meet on the first day of March for three months; Article 107 allowed an extension of one month if petitioned to do so by the king or by a two-thirds vote of the deputies. Bentham declared that this time span was surely too brief and would permit misrule particularly in the most distant provinces. Bentham saw the requisites of apt legislation as "1. To legislators, receipt of adequate information of the mischief, 2. Deliberation for choice of the remedy, 3. Application of the remedy."

23. "Art. 31—Por cada setenta mil almas de la población, compuesta como queda dicho en el artículo 29, había un Diputado de Cortes," from Serra (ed.), *Constituciones y Leyes*, 14; "Rid yourselves," 1820–22, in UCL, CLXVII, 179.
24. "Rid yourselves," 1820–22, in UCL, CLXVII, 185.
25. *Ibid.*

Yet, Bentham estimated that it took two to six months to get information from Creolia to Spain and the same amount of time to transmit the law "to the Seat of mischief" plus the time needed for the deliberation of the Cortes, king, and Council of State. "Result. Point made that in each or in first of the two years, nine months or at least eight months, there should be, during which, in legislation and many other operations to which Cortes alone is competent nothing shall be done. King and Council in full vigour."[26] Thence the mischief caused by the constitutional limit on the time that the Cortes could meet.

In summary, Bentham told the Spanish people he saw five principle ways that possession of overseas colonies vitiated the Spanish Constitution. These were:

1. By adding, to the number of your agents in the Cortes, others, with interests opposite to yours, and never removable by you.
2. By making, in a great variety of ways, addition to that mass of the matter of corruptive influence, which of itself, and without need of special acts of corruption, would at the long run, suffice to secure, on the part of your immediately deputed Agents, as well as the members of the Executive Government, the constant sacrifice of your interest in theirs.
3. By *doubling* the time, during which these your Agents continue *unremovable*, in how mischievous a degree soever violators of their trust.
4. By adding to the demand for the time of the Cortes: a time already insufficient for its proper and indispensable duties: thereby keeping the whole entangled business a labyrinth of confusion, into the windings of which no foreseeing eye would be able to penetrate.
5. By planting in those . . . regions with or without original design, a

---

26. "Art. 106—Las sesiones de las Cortes en cada año durarian tres meses consecutivos, dando principio el día 1° del mes de marzo" and "Art. 107—Las Cortes podrán prorrogar sus sesiones cuando más por otro mes en solos dos casos: primero, a petición del Rey; segundo, si las Cortes creyeron necesario por una resolución de las dos terceras partes de los diputados," from Serra (ed.), *Constituciones y Leyes*, 23; "Rid Yourselves," 1821, 1822, in UCL, VIII, 84; "J. B. to Spain," 1820, in UCL, VIII, 31.

necessary despotism, the reimportation of which into your peninsula would of all your imports from there be the most assured.[27]

Why should Spain rule Ultramaria? Why not Ultramaria rule
Spain? Bentham frequently used such extreme suggestions to emphasize his points, and this rather facetious possibility seemed to
intrigue him. He entitled one letter "The Claim of Ultramaria to
rule Spain Would be Better Than the Claim of Spain to Rule Ultramaria." The population of the overseas provinces was growing
much more rapidly than that of Spain. Since Spain's admitted
purpose under the constitution was the happiness of its people, or
the greatest happiness principle of Bentham, then the seat of the
government should be moved to Ultramaria and Spain could look
to Spanish America for relief. Whatever objections as to the difficulties of such a change Bentham countered with the example of
the movement of the Portuguese Court to Brazil during the Napoleonic era. While he did not advocate this radical move, he
thought it would be more profitable to Spain and less mischievous
to both Spain and Ultramaria.[28]

Bentham energetically argued that Ultramaria did not profit
Spain in the least. Taxes, the major source of revenue from Ultramaria, would become impossible to collect. The constitution, Article 8, provided equality of the proportional taxation without ex-
ception or privilege. If the people of a province believed their taxes
were out of proportion, they would appeal because everyone according to Article 373 had the right of memorial to king and
Cortes, whenever they felt the consitution was not being complied
with. Thus, they would not pay. He carried his argument further:
"With what face can your rulers call upon them to deprive themselves of a maravedi for their or for your use? Any more then they
could call upon you to do the likes for them. . . . With what face
can your rulers call upon them to receive bad commodities to the
exclusion of superior ones, dearer ones to the exclusion of cheaper
ones, in no other view than the hope that in some way or other you

27. "J. B. to Spain," 1820, in UCL, VIII, 121.
28. "Rid yourselves," 1820–22, in UCL, CLXVII, 192, 197, 251.

or they may receive at their expense a benefit which they cannot obtain or are ashamed or afraid to demand in a direct way!"[29]

Bentham closed this argument by stating categorically that, with such security against taxation, a share in the Spanish Cortes, as then constituted, or in any new fashion, would not change their views on taxation. Bentham held that Articles 335 and 324 gave to the Provincial Deputation (the government of the provinces), the right to approve taxes. "Of their functions, the first is to approve the quota of contributions assessed by the Cortes or the province. Thus no taxes will be generally collected, and if they were, they should according to the Constitution, be used for only the military force of Spain." If equality between Spain and Ultramaria was to be maintained, Spain would not profit. If this equality be violated, "union and peace none: instead of profit war expense. Vain all attempts to disguise the inequality, the coercion, by any form given to it: direct or indirect, tax will still be tax. . . . Imposed on all, a burden will be felt and resisted by all: imposed on the influential few, it will be imposed on them whose facilities for resistance are greatest."[30]

The sole means, then, for Spain to receive revenue from Ultramaria was "despotism and expense: military despotism and otherwise needless expense. Having no power, any of them, by any civil force at their disposal to secure for transmission to Spain a single maravedi, either all hopes of profit in this shape from Spanish America must be abandoned, or the Governors must be provided, each of them with a military force . . . of such strength, as should afford a sufficient promise, of overmatching any force, that seems likely to be opposed to them." If profit before was doubtful, how could it now be possible? "But the mischief lies not in the waste of money, but in the despotism which makes the Constitu-

29. "Art. 8—Tambien está obligado todo español, sin distinción alguna, a contribuir en proporción de sus haberes, para los gastos del Estado," from Serra (ed.), *Constituciones y Leyes*, 10; "Rid yourselves," 1820–22, in UCL, CLXVII, 142, 230.

30. "Rid Yourselves," 1821–1822, in UCL, VIII, 75. "Art. 335—1°. Intervenir y aprobar el repartimiento hecho a las pueblos de las contribuciones que hubieron cabido a la provincia," from Serra (ed.), *Constituciones y Leyes*, 52; "J. B. to Spain," 1820, in UCL, VIII, 37; "Rid yourselves," 1820–22, in UCL, CLXVII, 162.

tion an imposture. Instead of the new freedom which it professed to establish in both hemispheres, it reestablished in the Americas and thence in the European, the despotism which it professes to have drawn out from both."[31]

Bentham contended that even if the Creoles desired to stay with Spain, such union remained harmful to the Spanish people. The hope for money and troops from Ultramaria and the gratification from the power of dominion were all illusory expectations; the true result was pernicious. "To pursue the dominion would be to sacrifice the substance of internal security in pursuit of a shadow. For the chance of imposing the yoke of your rulers on your fellow sufferers will you submit to that you have just been liberated from . . . the danger from them is already present; the utmost profit expectable from the dominion is uncontrovertably distant; while struggling for it, what is to become of the exhausted body?" On the other hand, emancipation would bring many advantages. Because of the bonds of language, religions, laws, and customs, Spain's trade with her former colonies would greatly increase. "Bad must be Spanish goods and venders, not to have the preference: Money will thus flow in, without penal laws."[32]

In any case, since the same body can be in only one place at one time, be it man, ship, cannon, horse, money, how could Spain afford an army large enough to reconquer Mexico, Peru, the Philippines, and Cuba and at the same time defend itself against the "irregular depredations of African Mohammedans" and the opposition of European Christians? And the Spanish people alone through their taxes would pay for the army that reconquered America because taxes could not be collected in the rebellious provinces. Added to the expenses was the question of the army itself. Aware of immediate cause of the Revolution of 1820 in Spain, Bentham pointed out the attitude of soldiers who "feel averse to be banished to pestilential climes, to kill, maim, wound, impoverish unoffending kinsmen at such vast distances." If they did not like such an idea under the old absolutist government,

---

31. "J. B. to Spain," 1820, in UCL, VIII, 100.
32. *Ibid.*, 53, 22; "Rid yourselves," 1820–22, in UCL, CLXVII, 144.

they would like it even less now. Therefore, the Spanish government must change its policy.[33]

As is likely to happen in any document written over a period of time, Bentham occasionally used seemingly contradictory arguments in his efforts to push the Spanish people to emancipate their colonies. For example, he contended that Spain had only one enemy by land, France, which was no threat because of frugality and the memory of Spain's guerrillas, and one by sea, England, from whom Spain was "secure by her exclusive privilege." Therefore, Spain needed no navy except to protect Ultramaria, but Ultramaria thronged with potential enemies, the savage or barbarous, as well as the civilized, England, France, Portugal, and the Netherlands. "True, against U.S. you are saved by their long-suffering, without need of means of defense." Spain's sole strength lay with the guerrillas; of money, "the sinews of external war," Spain had none. Yet he argued just the opposite view when he claimed that Spain was menaced by "so many undisguised and threatening enemies," the Quadruple Alliance, ready to drag Spain back to the days of absolute monarchy. Should Spain risk the substance of internal security and independence for nothing better than a "perfectly indeterminate profit, from a most exhausting expenditure, certain and immediate. The struggle would all the while be taking its uncertain course. But what, in the meantime, would become of the exhausted body, by which all the exertions would be made?"[34]

These comments on empire, Bentham emphasized, were addressed not to the Spanish rulers but to the Spanish people, because the people themselves held the supreme constitutive power. Thus his words stressed the impact of continued dominion on the people, that is, the subject many, and their lives. The sole gainers in such arrangements were the functionaries, executive and legislative, who through the power and money from such an enterprise

---

33. "Rid yourselves," 1820–21, in UCL, CLXVII, 267; "Emancipation Spanish," 1820, in UCL, VIII, 49. See also page 204 of "Rid yourselves," 1820–22.

34. "Rid Yourselves," 1821, 1822, in UCL, VIII, 65, 122. See also "Rid yourselves," 1820–21, in UCL, CLXVII, 249, 191.

corrupted the supposed safeguards for Spain and Ultramaria, "forming not a bar but a cloak/cover to misrule."[35]

Bentham reasoned that the rulers then would be the sole gainers from such extended control, their profit being large but not sufficient to help the people in general. While some might view Bentham's argument as sowing seeds of dissension between the subject many and the ruling few, he replied to the charge by saying he was only indicating the danger from the strong to the weak anywhere and the necessity of dissension if war was to be prevented or made to cease. He further raised the question of whether it was the duty of the subject many to obey a government "in which the interest of the ruling few is in point blank opposition to that of the subject many if there was any means to avoid it." Without answering the question directly Bentham moved to a discussion of how the United States had solved this problem for forty years.[36]

The problem of the ruling few, as Bentham saw it, was that their interest, being particular, differed from the universal. This led Bentham to a detailed discussion of corruptive influence. This self-interest would result in not only the actual end of one man enjoying the use of his influence but also the corruption that comes from the hopeful expectation of such influence. Money and patronage, Bentham continued, always corrupt irremovable functionaries. To say, for instance, that money does not corrupt officials "is to say, that, when applied to them, water will not moisten them, fire warm them, or arsenic poison them." Irremovable functionaries would always convert the whole mass of "instruments of felicity" to a group of instruments for their own pleasure.

In Spain, Bentham suggested, under its constitution the subject many might succeed in eventually removing the ruling few, but such an outcome belonged to the future not the present. Thus the best course of action was to limit as much as possible the sources of corruptive influence available to the ruling few, specifically then: "Rid yourselves of Ultramaria." This might be the propitious moment for such action by the subject many, Bentham

35. "Rid Yourselves," 1821, 1822, in UCL, VIII, 86.
36. "Rid Yourselves," 1820–22, in UCL, CLXVII, 85.

continued, because, "the ruling few may, for a time, endure to regard themselves as standing in need of the support of the subject
many, for . . . common safety" as well as securing their own positions. This corruptive influence would eventually produce in the
representatives of the Cortes a corruptive obsequiousness because
these representatives might harbor hopes of delayed rewards for
their Cortes services when they were no longer representatives
there.[37]

Bentham devoted the major portion of these letters to attempts
to convince the Spanish people that they should freely and immediately grant independence to their American colonies. In the por-
cess of these arguments, however, Bentham also pointed out to
them the effects of this liberation on Spain. Using figures he admitted were imaginary, he illustrated the value, the profit, of total
emancipation, because partial emancipation meant the ratio of
expense to profit was increasing. No half measures, he argued,
should be allowed for any reason, for "by no alleged probability of
anarchy etc. in Creolia in consequence of emancipation, could re-
tention be justified." Even with such arguments as, "But our dear
kinsmen! You see the state of anarchy, you see the state of misery
into which some of them are plunged," by the withdrawal of the
benefits of Spain's good government, would Bentham deny the
overseas colonies such assistance? Indeed so, for to take them back
would mean hurting the Spanish people and emptying its treasury. On the other hand not relinquishing control because of so
called "honour" would be "senseless, ungrounded and false. By any
such relinquishment so far from your being lowered in the esteem
of other nations, I see you raised." Such full measures would save
the Spaniards from the mischief of war. Bentham argued that if
Spain kept striving to maintain control over them, they would
cease to be like Spain; if Spain desisted, they would be Spain's
imitator even as Naples was. Naples could be a lesson in honour;
from it Spain had reaped "a harvest of unexampled, of the only
pure joy." Thus for honour in the eyes of France, England, and the
United States, Spain must emancipate her colonies.[38]

37. *Ibid.*, 87; "Rid Yourselves," 1821, 1822, in UCL, VIII, 87.
38. "Rid Yourselves," 1821, 1822, in UCL, VIII, 88, 123; "J. B. to Spain," in UCL,

To make such a sacrifice more acceptable, Bentham recommended that Spain observe other nations' similar actions. Several of the Anglo-American states had given up land to the central government, many both voluntarily and spontaneously. This act brought them esteem and praise. Moving on to less willing emancipations, Bentham pointed out time and time again England's failure in keeping her thirteen North American colonies under her control, and suggested that Spain learn from that example. "England, with her vast resources, could not prevail against her Creoles, not 1/5 of her population. In your distress, can your rulers prevail over Ultramaria, more populous than you." Again, "Against less than 3 millions of Americans, the power of England failed. Can Spain succeed better against 12 millions or more? In the teeth of those principles which . . . she is professing." Bentham mentioned France's experience with Santo Domingo briefly, but he preferred to concentrate on the English example. Loss of empire, he emphasized, did not mean loss of profit. In England's case just the opposite was true. "The trade between Great Britain and the American United States is greater, in a prodigious degree, than it was before they shook off their independence. It began to increase immediately after the recognition of their independence." He documented this statement by quoting figures from Adam Seybert's *Statistical Annals* (Philadelphia, 1818) showing that the average trade for three years ending in 1773 was no more than £3,064,843. The year following the granting of independence, 1784, trade had jumped to £3,359,864. Such an increase, he suggested, would occur in Spain's trade with her former American colonies. Thus the ties of profit as well as a common language, religion, ancestry, and customs, would bind Spain and Ultramaria closer together after independence. He added, as was his wont, that the "fandango may remain after all laws and Constitution changed."[39]

VIII, 24. See similar argument Bentham used in urging Mexico to grant land for Junctiana Canal, Chapter VI herein.

39. "Rid Yourselves," 1821, 1822, in UCL, VIII, 122. Bentham cited six examples of states ceding land to the United States government (See *ibid.*, 77, 92, 104, 110–11; "Rid Yourselves," 1820, *ibid.*, 54, and "Rid yourselves," 1820–22, in UCL, CLXVII, 156.)

In a manuscript dated July 25, 1818, entitled "Emancipation Preface," Bentham wrote, "Among the propositions demonstrated in this address is this to wit that to the people of the country to which it belongs distant dependence is in every instance a source of net loss." The climax to this argument came when he asked the Spanish to estimate their expenses if the colonies were freed; also to estimate the cost for each dependency kept including military land service, sea service, civil service, judiciary, and those officials in charge of the general superintendence of the colonies; and to add to this the estimated cost of regaining dependencies already virtually lost and the expenses of retaining them; finally, to compare the total of the second and third with the annual receipts expected from each province. This would show the Spanish people, Bentham contended, what the colonies would be costing them.[40]

As Bentham's ideas developed, he began to consider the proper means of relinquishment of the colonies. He outlined the possible ways Spain might end her control over Ultramaria. The mode might likely be determined by the degree of subjection of the various provinces, *i.e.*, whether Spanish control was "(1) completely cast off, (2) contested, (3) uncontested."[41] The terms of such action might be either gratuitous or for a price. The latter would be paid by the inhabitants in the form of redemption money or by a foreign power as purchase money. Bentham listed the advantages of the gratuitous plan as the one most extensively applicable, most surely effective and most honorable. It would, he pointed out, be impossible to extract money from those who had cast off their connection with Spain or from foreign countries for them. But freely granting them independence would bring honor to Spain from them and all nations. In those areas where Spanish control was contested, redemption money would be difficult to find, but even if money was available Article 8 of the constitution declared *equal-*

40. "Emancipation Preface," 1818, in UCL, VIII, 6; "Emancipation Spanish: Summary of a work," 1820, in UCL, CLXII, 26.
41. "Rid Yourselves," 1821, 1822, in UCL, VIII, 112. On April 2, 1822, Bentham changed his terminology to read "1. Independent, 2. still subject, 3. contesting subjection," (p. 105).

ity of rights, according to Bentham, and thus demanding money of them was contrary to the constitution. Thus any money from foreigners for purchase must consider the province's willingness to be sold.[42]

As to the last section, those areas where subjection was uncontested, here possibly a foreign power might be willing to pay Spain for its claims. Perhaps recalling the fairly recent Adams-Onís Treaty which allowed the United States to take over Florida, Bentham stressed that only the United States' president would be interested because the land was continguous and retainable without additional expense. The only territories, however, that the United States might want were those between the Mississippi and the Pacific. Ownership of the islands might intrigue the president but his constituents would not allow him to buy them because of the additional expense in fleets and armies to protect them and because of "increasing his patronage and rearing an Aristrocracy, headed by him." The advantages of the United States purchasing any part of Creolia included:

1. To Spanish subject many, pecuniary easement.
2. To Creoles, good government and content.
3. To a third party, advantage.
4. To Spaniards, pure and unexampled glory.

Bentham suggested then, "To a well governed neighboring Confederacy, Sale of the province, i.e. of the unappropriated land in it, with transfer of the province to the Confederacy: viz. to U.S.A." Bentham saw precedents for such action on the part of Spain in the sale of Louisiana for money to Napoleon and the sale of Florida in satisfaction of debts.

Transfer of Ultramarian provinces Bentham suggested would follow this pattern: Spanish rulers would ask the United States for money and receive in return Spanish claims; the two nations then would join together in an attempt to get the provinces to agree to the transaction. Using the same thought he expressed often in his canal proposal, Bentham had Spain saying to the United States,

42. "Rid Yourselves," 1821, 1822, in UCL, VIII, 112.

"You are used to take States to nurse, and when of age, admitt [*sic*] them into partnership. Do so by this province." The United States must agree, however, not to take them without their consent. Evidently the consent was to come by some sort of vote. "After adequate notification, and time for consideration, and counter notification of dissent, regard non-dissentients as assentients. Bare majority of *such* assentients would not be sufficient. To determine what would be, a joint task for benevolence and prudence: suppose, in the long run, dissentients a majority, such transfer would not be free admission but war and conquest."[43]

In the event the United States did take over former Spanish colonies, Bentham considered the possibility of incompatible difference between the United States and the lands to the south. He found none. The difference in religion would be no difficulty as evidenced in the previous transfer of Florida and the existence of Catholics in Maryland. The language difference was one obstacle, "but not insuperable"; here Bentham cited the example of the Netherlands. Should the Spanish colonies refuse the offer of the United States, no one would have lost face or honor.

In a later reworking of this idea, Bentham suggested that Spanish-constituted authorities invite comparable authorities of the United States to send commissions or commissioners to Madrid, Washington, London, or to the capital of the Ultramarian province in question. The inhabitants and rulers of the province would be notified to form a similar commission which would meet with the others. At an appointed time the province would decide on the recommendations of the commissions by either complete adoption, complete rejection, or adoption with amendments. Such action would take the form of a memorial; when the memorial was received, a constitution would be drawn up modeled on the United States or Spanish one. The commissioner, meantime, would appoint functionaries to act as a provisional government until the constitution was completed.[44]

Throughout Bentham saw cession of Ultramaria to the United

---

43. *Ibid.*, 113; "Emancipation Spanish," 1820, *ibid.*, 44.
44. "Rid Yourselves," 1821, 1822, in UCL, VIII, 103.

States to be in keeping with the basic maxim of utilitarianism. Bentham, perhaps anticipating manifest destiny, particularly urged the Spanish settlements on the Pacific (he does not say how far south) to join the United States, promising them the security of peace and amity. Self government in any Spanish colonies was not an actuality yet, merely a prospect. Thus, "for industry, by Solomon, the sluggard was sent to the ant; for self-government nations should be sent to the U. S." He suggested that the Pacific provinces join the union as Louisiana had; as to any compensation from the United States, Bentham once more avoids the subject: "Whether any money, and what would be given *now* by the U.S. J. B. has no means of judging."[45] Should Spain need to look for a purchaser other than the United States, Bentham faintheartedly suggested England, but England was no competitor because of its own retrenchment. Russia, of course, was no contender either, even for possible conquests, because of her debility and distance.[46]

Another suggestion that Bentham made to Spain in regard to the United States was a plan for what he termed, "conjunct mediation." In this plan the United States would send commissioners as they had to Buenos Aires and Chile, and Spain would do likewise. These commissioners jointly would help Ultramarian provinces to draw up their plans of government. Bentham assumed that many provinces would not want commissioners from monarchial Spain alone, but along with representatives of a republican state they would be accepted. He predicted that many would choose the Spanish Constitution as a model but without the monarchy. This constitution, Bentham argued, would fall apart without the monarchy, but a change allowing amendments would save the constitution from collapse. Thus what Spain could not do as a master it might do as a friend through a mediatory commission. If the conjunct mediation failed, "nothing is sacrificed or hazarded." And Spanish America, Bentham felt, must suffer the consequences.[47]

45. *Ibid.*, 104, 114.
46. *Ibid.*, 102, 113.
47. "Emancipation Spanish," 1820, in UCL, VIII, 43.

Bentham used every means at his disposal to convince the Spaniards of the necessity of freeing Ultramaria for the sake of Spain. While he was evidently interested in the fate of Ultramaria, he stressed in his letters to Spain that the "sole present, direct, and ultimate object" of his regard was Spain's welfare. He played heavily on his reputation in Spain.

My game deep: for 50 years labour, from you sweetest hopes These I stake, to rid you of your most oppressive burden. He who feels anger, by the warmth of it let him judge of the zeal that could expose a man to it. When heard, take from me your good opinion if you wean, and thus strangle me.[48]

Bentham realized that his efforts to convince Spain to willingly free her colonies would probably not succeed. He wrote to Edward Blaquiere on June 5, 1820, "At this time I am hard at work upon an almost hopeless attempt: that of persuading the rulers in Spain, whoever they are, to emancipate all Spanish America, even though said Spanish America were down upon her knees to beg to be retained." Yet he persisted. He sent a copy of his first article on the subject, the French *Emancipate Your Colonies*, to Rivadavia in 1820, saying that he had omitted reference to corruptive influence from this first attempt. He urged Rivadavia to use it: "But you, Sir—you, whose interest in the matter is so immediate, and whose knowledge of the subject is so commanding—how could your talents at this crisis be so worthily employed, as by the application of them to this great question? viz. either by an original or independent work, or by a translation into Spanish, of the little Tract in question, if found worthy of it; with comments, applying the arguments to the present case; or in short, devoting those talents to a something between both, or including both."[49]

In a later letter to Rivadavia (June 13, 1822) Bentham said he was sending to Mexico by one of their deputies to the Cortes "a manuscript copy of a paper containing in the form of titles, the copies of a series of Letters, addressed to the Spanish people—*not*

48. "Rid Yourselves," 1821, 1822, in UCL, VIII, 70, 72.
49. Bowring (ed.), *Works*, X, 513–15.

to their rulers under the title of *Rid Yourselves of your Ultramaria."*
He also informed the porteño that he had at the request of José J.
de Mora, Spanish liberal political leader and author, sent such
parts that "promised to be of most use" to him in his efforts to win
Spanish American independence. Likewise he had sent to Manuel
Fernandez Thornay, "the first man" of the Portuguese Cortes, "the
finished part" of his letters because he had said in the Cortes, "If it
be agreeable to the Brazilians to remain united with us, so much
the better: but if not, it is not with my good will that any endeavour would be made to force them to it." Thornay reacted so favorably to Bentham's comments that he put it immediately into
the hands of a translator so "that those who think with him on
that subject might make the most of it." But, two years after urging Rivadavia to take some action concerning his ideas, he
changed his views and wrote, "To you in your position, it could at
the utmost be nothing more than a matter of curiosity; it could
not be of any real use."[50]

So while others might doubt the value of such arguments as
Bentham made to Spain on behalf of independence, Bentham took
his ideas quite seriously and expected or at least hoped that some
others would, too. In a letter to Bolívar dated December 24, 1820,
Bentham said, "I have, for some time, been labouring, might and
main, in the joint service of yourself and your till-of-late inhuman
enemy. I say, in your joint service: for, the title of my work, is 'Rid
Yourselves of Ultramaria'." He promised the Liberator to enclose
in the letter the titles of the sections, and continued in his self
aggrandizing fashion, "Regarding this as the greatest service, I or
any body, or all the world together, could render to Spain, I stake
my whole credit in that country, for whatever chance I have of
rendering it. If rendered by any body, it must be by me: for the
attachment to that most oppressive of all their burthens, except
the so lately mitigated despotism, is no less blind and deaf than it
is extensive."[51]

50. Bentham to Rivadavia, June 13, 1822, in UCL, XII, 387.
51. Bentham to Bolívar, December 24, 1820, in UCL, CLXIII, 25.

Five

LIBERTY OF THE PRESS

FOR THE ACHIEVEMENT OF HIS GOALS in Spanish America Bentham believed a free press was essential. What appears to be the first document he drew up especially for Spanish America dealt with this problem. This "Proposed Law for the establishment of Liberty of the Press in Venezuela" was written in 1808,[1] and in August and September of 1810 he added the "Particular Codes" which would implement the proposed law.[2] At the time that Bentham wrote these codes, he was particularly concerned with liberty of the press in England, especially the libel law which he thought "incompatible with English liberties."[3] But liberty of the press had long been a major concern. As early of 1789 in the series of essays on "Principles of International Law," Bentham had listed liberty of the press as another of the six measures he recommended for creating international law and eliminating war.[4]

These two Spanish American documents, along with his proposal for the Junctiania Canal, constitute the most extensive, substantive work that he prepared solely for Spanish America. As in all his writing he was quite ready, indeed anxious, to share these

1. "Proposed Law for the establishment of Liberty of the Press in Venezuela," in UCL, XXVI, 2–11. The Milne catalog dates this document 1808. The date is not evident on the document itself, which is today fragmentary, faded, and frayed at the edges much more so than most of the Bentham manuscripts. Each page is written in four small columns as though it was an outline for later expansion.

2. "Venezuela—proposed law for securing the liberty of the Press," 1810, in UCL, XXI, 7–56.

3. Halévy, *The Growth of Philosophic Radicalism*, 256.

4. Bowring (ed.), *Works*, II, 546.

documents with other countries who, he believed, might easily adapt them to their needs.

Francisco de Miranda had asked Bentham to draw up a law regarding the free press. Bentham in telling his cousin, Dr. Mulford, of his decision to go to Venezuela rather than Mexico, remarked that Miranda "took with him the draught of a law, which, at his solicitation, I drew up for the establishing of the liberty of the press."[5]

Bentham felt that a free press was a sine qua non for any utilitarian state, but he was particularly aware of the difficulties faced in drafting a law that would protect this liberty. In a letter to Blanco White, Bentham commented on the appointment of a committee of eight by the Spanish Cortes for drawing up a similar law:

At the request of a common friend of ours [Miranda], so it happens, that I have of late been occupied—I am ashamed to say for what length of time—in drawing up a Code upon that subject, including what to me seem the necessary explanations. Though the principles were fully settled, the text was not quite finished when he left this country; but as much was finished and put into his hands, as there could be an practical use for, for some time to come. He had been several times attacking me on that subject. My answer was, that the accomplishment of it was precisely the most difficult of all problems discoverable in the field of legislation; and amongst other reasons for this, comprised in it: that, in a word, in my view of the matter, everything else within that field was child's play in comparison of it. Such was the difficulty I actually found: accordingly, without its being yet quite finished, about two months of my time were completely occupied by my attempt.[6]

Quite naturally he then volunteered to send a copy of his proposed law for Venezuela to White for Spain's use because, "You know, without my telling you, the latitude for which my draught was calculated; but a very trifling alteration would, I believe, suffice for rendering it as fit for the purpose now in question, as for

5. *Ibid.,* X, 458.
6. *Ibid.,* 456.

that which is was designed." But Bentham understood the depth of the animosity Miranda felt toward Spain and mentioned that Miranda would surely have mixed feelings over sharing with Spain "a work which he had in some measure been entitled to consider as his own." In spite of this, however, Bentham quickly dismissed such thoughts, saying that Miranda, if all went well, would have already put the law into effect in Venezuela before a copy of White's paper *Español*, telling of Spain's use of his document, could possibly reach his hand. Bentham finally resolved his dilemma, however, by stating, "Whatever, if any, may be the value of it, I have too high a sense of his liberality to suppose him capable of considering it a proper subject for engrossment."[7]

The "Proposed Law" dealt primarily with the overall value and necessity of liberty of the press and the means by which this could be secured. The second document, the "Particular Codes," established safeguards against the abuses of this liberty by the press itself.

The press included, in Bentham's view, "not only the printing press but all means of forming visible and permanent signs of ideas." The press as thus defined must be free from any required government license because, while prevention is generally thought of as preferable to punishment, in this case "mischief by bondage is unlimited, of abuse limited and restrictable." Such power of licensing would be much too great for any single individual, for it required "super-human probity and intelligence," and gave the licenser supreme powers. "He condemns without hearing the author to a severe punishment, the world to a boundless loss. Magnet, Opium, Vaccination or the Bible what if lost for want of a licenser."[8]

Thus the press must be free of restriction, and political criticism must be lawful "saving regard to foreign powers." Oral or written discourse in relation to public affairs must be legal with the right to express approval or disapproval with or without basis

7. *Ibid.*, 456–57. Engrossment is used by Bentham to mean monopoly.
8. "Proposed Law for the establishment of Liberty of the Press in Venezuela," in UCL, XXVI, 6.

in fact. Bentham further stressed that liberty of the press would mean the circulation of newspapers and books containing political criticism without government interference provided they contained the printer's or publisher's name or had not been prohibited by judicial sentence. Those that did not contain political criticism were to be free from antecedent restraint except for those that might be included in a prohibited list duly drawn up by the representatives of the people.

Although Bentham revealed great faith in popular government, he specifically stated, "Popularity of the form of government [is] no adequate succedaneum to freedom of the press." Bentham formulated that if in the exercise of such freedom an agent of the people be unjustly aspersed he had two remedies, self-defense by the press and judicial prosecution. The judicial proceeding in such cases was to be public, as a means of securing and maintaining the intellectual fitness of the judge, or securing diligence ("Eye of the public a *spur*"), and of securing probity, ("Eye of the public, a bridle"). Thus: "To a free constitution a free press is necessary. If by the member of the government the people be kept from the necessary means of judging of the fitness of public men and their measures, it were better for them not to have any part in the placing or displacing public men."[9]

The role of liberty of the press in a free society thus became evident. It served as a means of eliminating the causes of misrule: sinister interest, ignorance, faulty information, error from fallacious reasoning, and error from lack of ability.

The sinister interest of which Bentham later wrote so much in his letters to the Spanish people on emancipation was private and separate interest as opposed to public interest. Under a monarch, sinister interest abounds; "it is only in a popular government that sinister interest finds an adequate check." But "with information comes opposition: conjunct opposition, by which . . . sinister interest [is] thwarted." Liberty of the press provided such information and provided at the same time the remedy to ignorance. Similarly,

9. *Ibid.*

error from false facts and false arguments would be eliminated by exposure to information. Lack of ability would also be remedied by a free press's giving facts and arguments a general exposure. Bentham here referred to Charles IV, remarking that liberty of the press in Spain during his reign would probably have caused the removal of Godoy, the Prince of Peace, from his position of great power which he used to further his own private (hence sinister) interest. Thus, Bentham concluded, for all these causes of misrule, "liberty of the press is in all these cases an indispensable, in some the only, remedy."[10]

With the value and necessity of liberty of the press clearly established, Bentham turned to the problem of how this liberty could be secured. The government could not prevent the dissemination of facts, for "liberty excludes antecedent restraint." But the absence of governmental licensing and previous restraint could not alone guarantee liberty of the press. This freedom, Bentham argued, must still be protected from engrossment and partiality. The possibility of monopoly control, he pointed out, comes not only from government control but from the concentration of the power of the press in the hands of only a few. Bentham feared that if one individual succeeded in becoming master of the press, he would sooner or later be master of the government because he had the means of attack and the means of spreading false and fallacious information concerning the government and his enemies while he printed information favorable to himself and his interest. Such monopoly from this erstwhile master of the government would be like "a *trial* carried on orally, advocates and witnesses gagged." Bentham continued, "Besides being tormented by him in this character of the master of the government, opponents would be aspersed, and destroyed in reputation by him in his character of master of the press." The more presses a nation had the less likely engrossment by one or more individuals was to occur. Bentham reminded his readers, however, that presses abounded in Britain and Anglo-America but even so "the mischief of a sort of

10. *Ibid.,* 10–11.

partial engrossment has been felt." How much more so would it be felt in an area such as Venezuela where presses for some time would be few. Thus the press would be free only insofar as it would be protected not only against the constituted authorities but also against individual engrossers. Bentham was not clear as to how he planned to prevent such monopoly control.

Even if the press should be free of restraint from both antecedent restriction and engrossment, Bentham agreed that impartiality was not thereby ensured, for "by law even impartiality cannot be enforced." But if a public man's reputation was maligned, the law could establish methods for giving him an opportunity for rebuttal. The details of this recommendation he deferred to the particular code for private editors, but Bentham recommended that the government, "require such observances as without too much vexation shall render partiality as difficult as possible."[11]

To help ensure impartiality, Bentham proposed the creation of a government newspaper which would "serve as an appellate Judicatory," being obliged to insert all notices of transgression by the press. While private editors could not be expected to insert all papers sent to them, they should at least mention them. But government newspaper editors, who because of their position would be jealously and universally watched, should be required to take an oath of office that would impose the moral sanction on them to ensure impartiality in the handling of papers received by them for insertion in the paper.

If liberty of the press could be thus secured, protected from antecedent restraint, monopoly, and partiality, what action had to be taken to prevent abuses of this liberty by the press itself? Bentham saw two "modes of transgression the press especially the Newspaper . . . is apt to (be) preeminently subservient to." These were false reports to produce gain or loss and injurious aspersions on reputations. Bentham did not develop the first of these ideas but simply stated that the newspaper could more effectively produce gain or loss through false reports than any other instrument.

11. *Ibid.*, 9–12.

He gave much consideration, however, to aspersions of reputation, particularly whether the reputation would be injured, whether the truth was violated, and whether moral balance was evident. He was especially concerned with the slander of public officials because it involved an abuse of the liberty of political criticism. Since popular government required that its citizens have access to information for forming opinions of public men, proposed laws, and institutions, the criticism of public men became a necessity. However, attacks on reputation must not violate truth and decorum. Bentham felt that false statements tended toward deception and were conducive to misrule, whereas violations of decorum produced only bad effects. Evidence could easily establish the truth or lack of truth, but how was decorum to be decided since no determinate bounds existed establishing the limits of decorum? Bentham advised that punishment for indecorum be carefully limited by law "lest this liberty be converted into a snare." Thus "for the double purpose of doing what can be done towards securing the best use of the press with reference to political information, and *preventing abuse*; it is necessary to give definitions of the offenses by which reputation is aspersed together with appropriate *satisfaction* and *punishment*."[12]

To this end as well as others, Bentham dedicated his "Particular Codes." The objectives of this body of laws he listed as

1. Prevention of press abuses
2. of d° [prevention of abuses] of political criticism
3. Minimizing responsibility in point of extent
4. Reconciling eventual responsibility with the secrecy necessary to liberty
5. Securing liberty of political discussion against the partiality exercisible by means of engrossment
6. Securing correspondents thereby against rejection or delay.[13]

In title II of the "Proposed Law" Bentham had listed the Particular Codes as follows:

12. *Ibid.*, 8, 7.
13. *Ibid.*

Ch. 1   Printers Law
Ch. 2   Bookseller's Law
Ch. 3   Newspaper Editor & Law
Ch. 4   Government Newspapers Editors & Law
Ch. 5   Newspaper Correspondents & Law

When he developed these codes, however, he changed the titles somewhat:

Ch. 1   Printers Law
Ch. 2   Booksellers and Publishers Law
Ch. 3   Laws concerning the Printers, Conductors and Proprietors of Newspapers and other periodical political works
Ch. 4   Government Newspaper
Ch. 5   Newspaper (Communicators) Correspondents Law

This fifty-page document, unlike the "Proposed Law," is dated. The dates in August and September of 1810 correspond to Bentham's comments to Blanco White about the two months he spent writing for Miranda. In these laws Bentham attempted to spell out in minute detail the responsibilities of all those who were associated with the press. The Printer's Law (the briefest of all, being only two pages), required that the printer's name and address appear on every sheet of paper printed within the state. The printer bore responsibility for everything he printed and in any violation he became a co-offender and would be subject to punishment for the offense. Should he seek to avoid such difficulty by using another's name, such action would be deemed forgery and punished as such. Booksellers or publishers who distributed printed works bore responsibility as accomplices should they be aware of such forgery. However, should a publisher choose, he might substitute his name as publisher in place of that of the printer, thus assuming the liability as well as the liberty of political criticism which the printer had.[14]

Evidently thinking that Venezuelan authorities might fear the power of a free press in fomenting international crises, Bentham

14. "Venezuela—proposed law for securing the liberty of the Press," in UCL, XXI, 7, 10–11.

gave the executive of Venezuela the power to interdict any literary work printed or published in his state that was "deficient in the regard/respect due to the Sovereign power of any foreign state, or to any person in authority under such" government. This action might be taken at the request of "any accredited Agent of such foreign state." After the interdiction was fully publicized, anyone contributing to the circulation of such a work "may be subjected [to] any doom not exceeding in rigour the most rigourous of those herein ordained." However, by his use of the word "may," Bentham gave authorities the power without making it an ironclad rule.

In the Particular Codes Bentham defined newspapers and periodicals and carefully allocated responsibilities among those who produced them. Every printer of a newspaper or periodical Bentham termed "a Political Printer," subject to specific regulations. Newspapers he defined as those works whose object was "giving the most recent information of and concerning political work as they wish," while periodical newspapers were those that appeared at stated times and were always the same length. He included under the latter works periodicals which, while they might or might not contain news articles, did regularly contain political criticism. Bentham specifically defined political criticism as paragraphs containing opinions or advice on public conduct, administration, legislation, *etc.*

Bentham identified the printer as the person in command of the machinery by which newspapers were printed. He might also be the "conductor," that is, the one who wrote or selected the articles printed. If they were different persons, the printer was immediately responsible for what was printed, while the conductor was considered his servant unless by agreement between the owner, printer, and conductor, thereby relieving the printer of all responsibility save monetary. The proprietor of a newspaper was the one who paid the expenses, reaped the profits, and employed others as printer and conductor. His responsibility was established by law and except in "special or actual privity" was exempt from other liability. Names of any partners in such ventures, "co-proprietors," Bentham termed them, should be entered in a Secret Communication Register, which remained in the custody of the printer to be used only for judicial inquiry. Bentham stated in a paragraph curiously marked over by a large 22 that anyone might freely carry on the business of a newspaper printer or conductor/ publisher without obligation other than those contained in the Printer's Law.

The major goal in these attempts to structure a system in which the press would have relative freedom appears to be to guarantee to every interested citizen opportunities for commenting critically on the activities and actions of his government. This right of political criticism must be so protected that secrecy as to the author's identity could be concealed unless the criticism was in some way libelous or untrue. Then, by court order, the author's identity might be revealed. In the Particular Codes, Bentham established a system that he thought would effectively protect this right which he believed vital to popular government. He required that each paper printed in Venezuela have following the name and address of the printer the statement *"Open for impartial insertion of pieces of political criticism from correspondents declared or concealed."*[15]

Then Bentham constructed a method whereby he hoped to secure impartiality toward such correspondence. Each newspaper was required to have an "open communication" or "open correspondents book" in which a record was kept of all articles submitted to the paper. The entry for each should be made as soon as possible after receipt and should be given a number for the record. Bentham left the exact specifications to the Venezuelan authorities but he made parenthetical suggestions. The entry would contain the title, not to be more than (ten) words; if no title was listed, the printer would give it a title. The title would be followed by the first (four) words of the paper; the last (four) words; name of the communicator, whether real or fictitious "or subjoined by the Communicator," with his address if given; time, day, date re-

15. *Ibid.*, 12–16.

ceived, date of paper, if any listed, how received—printed or written, without saying which press or hand. This book was to remain
at the printer's office, available for inspection by anyone applying
for that purpose and paying the required fee. Bentham added that
the fee should be quite small since its sole purpose was to eliminate "wanton and vexatious application."[16] In addition to this record, the printer should write on some conspicuous part of every
paper thus received: the exact time he received it, and whether it
was by mail or hand. Should the person delivering it want acknowledgment of receipt from the printer, he might upon payment
of a fee receive a signed receipt.

In the next paper if possible, or the one following at the latest,
the printer must insert an account, in the prescribed manner, of
all communications received since his last such notice. If the communicator so requested, the printer might insert a sample of the
article not to exceed a specified number, say one hundred, words.
Should the communicator not make the selection, then the printer
might, taking care for "completeness to the sum and agreement,
as far as time and space will admit."[17]

Realizing that some such articles might lose their effectiveness
if printing was long postponed, Bentham, though he advocated
printing articles in the order received, allowed the printer lee-
way in accommodating those for which postponement would be
equivalent to frustration and rejection. The printer should mention those articles not included by stating his intentions in this
manner, "Insertion *declined* or Insertion *postponed.*" The latter
would be because of more immediate urgency. The printer should
inform his public, however, as to why he refused to print certain
articles. Three valid reasons were mentioned by Bentham: (1) contrary to law—indecorous, giving rise to delinquency, (2) superceded by prior communication on the same subject (3) or not
being in correct form for public eye or too incorrect in form.

In addition to the open communication book each printer's of-

16. *Ibid.,* 17–18. Bentham elsewhere used *correspondent* instead of *communicator.*
17. *Ibid.,* 20–21.

fice had to keep a secret communication book into which descriptions of all communications in which secrecy had been decreed along with the real name and description of the communicator were entered. Names of those requesting secrecy would not be divulged except under court order. To better assure secrecy of names, Bentham suggested they seal their names inside an envelope which should be given to the printer. When the seal was broken it would be the responsibility of the printer and he should enter his name and the time broken open. Any person who used a fictitious name for purposes of deceit would be considered punishable for forgery. Bentham justified the privilege of thus allowing persons to express views in the press without publicly revealing their names as simply a means of allowing everyone to express his views without fear of punishment.

Fearing an inconsistency in his arguments, Bentham stated that requiring printers and conductors to reveal their names in each publication did not inhibit their freedom of expression. When they did not wish to be known as the author of an article, they might use the system open to all citizens of entering their names in the secret communications book whose secrecy depended upon themselves.

Bentham believed his overall plan for ensuring the right of political criticism and its impartial publications would provide the interested public man with a means of discovering how much interest existed in a particular topic, and how well the public mind was developing in relation to the art and science of government, as well as the number of persons who agreed or disagreed with his views.

Still, in allowing the public and the press such latitude, Bentham realized the possibility that some might misuse it. He declared that any person who suffered wrongful defamation or vituperation in any newspaper could require the offending paper to print his intention to seek satisfaction of the communicator of such passage or the conductor or both as the case may be, in a court of law. Such intention should be in the form of a notice which contained the exact date of the paper, the page, and the first and last words of the offending passage. The second paragraph of the notice would read:

In respect of such wrong, it is therefore my intention to call you to account in due court of justice within ( ) months vig. as the day of (month) (year) or as soon after as conveniently may be at the (designate here the judicatory) at which time you or the person by whom the aforesaid passage was communicated to you, and who acknowledge himself as such are hereby summoned to appear.[18]

Bentham favored the joint responsibility of the printer and communicator for aspersions rather than the printer alone because the printer, if he alone was responsible, would hesitate to publish articles for fear of litigation, and thus political criticism would be discouraged and curtailed. Should the complainant fail to appear at the hearing, he must agree to pay the printer a fixed sum plus that which the court deemed proper to satisfy the printer's loss in time and trouble.

The oath or promise to be taken by the "Conductor as well as, or instead of the Printer" of the official government newspaper that Bentham had recommended in the "Proposed Law" took its final form in the Particular Codes. Taken as a whole, this summarizes Bentham's views about securing impartiality in the press. It began:

In the presence of (——) I. A. P. being by the choice of ( ) nominated to the office of Printer of the Government Gazette for the State of Venezuela do solemnly promise and declare as follows

1. That so long as I continue in possession of my said office, I will, to the best of my ability in the execution of the cause, do justice to all men alike, to high and to low, to rich and to poor (to those of one race and those of another race) not aspiring myself to be ——— by personal interest, by hope or by fear, or by favour or aversion towards any individual or class of men or party in the state.[19]

The oath continued with those qualities which Bentham thought should be stressed: impartiality, the ability to discern

18. *Ibid.*, 23.
19. *Ibid.*, 28.

what should be kept secret and what should be publicized, "uncorruption as to gifts" and to "advantage by intelligence," and finally impartiality as to choice, sample, and priority. He developed these ideas so that the oath included the adherence of the printer, in respect to insertion or rejection, to the public good, giving preference to the most important communications and those reflecting the greatest ability. However, impartiality was to be valued over ability as such and in cases where weak reasoning on one side was opposed by two strongly reasoned articles on the other, he should promise to print one article on each side. As for samples, he should promise to print that part that displayed the "matter of the paper to the best advantage." Priority would be given to the article that could least afford to be delayed, and all communications would be given the same publicity except those that by law should be kept secret.

In addition to these pledges, the printer or conductor should promise not to accept any gift or favors intended to influence his views or the views of any who worked for him. He should make known his suspicions of such in his paper. In addition such officials would promise not to take advantage of information that might have come their way to increase their own fortunes or decrease those of others.

Bentham felt the oath or promise was of such significance in securing liberty of the press that he recommended that newspaper conductors other than government newspaper conductors be allowed and encouraged to make this promise and for a fee should be given a certificate attesting to that fact.

Bentham saw the political newspaper printers in the state as the judges not only over individuals but over the government itself, since they decided what information about public affairs the people themselves were to have. Ultimately, he saw the printer of the government newspaper as "a sort of judge paramount over all these judges." On him fell the responsibility of dealing with injustice that might arise from other newspapers. The oath or promise would secure the probity of this official, protecting him against temptations from sinister interest of his own or others at the same time that it helped him understand his own duties. The government paper would insert notices of prosecutions for aspersions contained in other newspapers because it was larger, had greater circulation, and hopefully might prod by this action others' papers to do likewise. The government printer was likewise compelled to insert either in whole or part all political essays submitted to him in order to secure impartiality that might be limited by the printer's closeness to the government. Bentham stressed the value of such political criticism:

Nothing can be more desirable than that communications of this sort should increase and multiply. The greater the increase of them the broader and more compulsory will be the grounds for that choice of public men which the body of the people will so frequently be called upon to make. But of these communications the utility depends altogether upon the impartiality of the whole mass of them taken in the aggregate.[20]

Bentham explained why responsibility was laid on the printer in preference to the bookseller. Always interested in the facility of enforcing a law, he argued that placing the responsibility on the printer "reduces to its minimum the hardship imposed by law." The bookseller could hardly be expected to read every work he sold; he could, however, check each work for the name of the printer. The printer, on the other hand, read the material in the course of his work. Punishing the bookseller, too, would be punishing for disobedience when obedience was impossible.

These well-laid plans for the creation of a free press dedicated to promoting and developing popular government came to nothing. Francisco de Miranda, for whom Bentham had such high hopes, never had an opportunity to implement them. By the end of July, 1812, Miranda was a captive of the Spanish, never again to be free.[21]

But Bentham knew that his plans for Spanish America required a free press, and he persisted in his attempts to achieve his goal by one means or another. In a letter to Rivadavia on October

20. *Ibid.*, 48–52.
21. Robertson, *The Life of Miranda*, II, 180ff.

3, 1818, he remarked briefly about liberty of the press and its role in providing constitutional security and the fact that so often such liberty was due not to the guaranties of the law but the debility of the government.[22] He continued this theme in a letter to Bolívar in July and August of 1825, when he commented on the power of the press in England where daily newspapers and other periodicals were increasing daily the force of the tribunal of public opinion.[23]

Bentham was delighted by reports from his English friend Francis Hall. Hall wrote Bentham that he had founded a newspaper, the *Anglo-Colombian*, in Caracas using both Spanish and English "with the double object of creating a spirit of free discussion, and of disseminating correct information on the state of the country, through America, the colonies and I may say, the world." But, Hall reported, just as the paper was succeeding, he was ordered to go to "the seat of the Government as a military man." Such action, Hall insisted, did not upset him, "but the public would have it that it was to the principles advocated in my paper I was indebted for the pleasure of the journey." Even so, all was not lost. A company was formed to buy a press so that "the extinction of one Editor, like cutting off the Hydra's head, gave birth to twenty more." This was probably not a totally candid account of Hall's reaction to his transfer. However, Bentham learned the rest of the story from a letter of Hall's to William Empson, a copy of which is in the Bentham manuscripts with the heading in Bentham's hand, "To be seen but not published J. B." Hall began by telling his friend of his impending trip to Bogotá "in obedience to an order of the Government, which has no taste for free newspapers. I know this to be the real cause of my journey." But, as he had told Bentham, his work would continue: "The example of a free newspaper has roused a spirit of bold inquiry which will never be laid but in blood." He told of the formation of a society of Caracanians formed to continue the publication of the *Anglo-Colombian*. "They have bought a new English printing apparatus, and

22. Bentham to Rivadavia, October 3, 1818, in Add. MSS 33545, BM.
23. O'Leary (ed.), *Memorias del General O'Leary*, XII, 278–79.

the government by its zeal to put down one editor has raised up fifty."[24]

Bentham, within a week of the receipt of his letter from Hall, wrote to him and sent it by Leander Miranda, the son of Francisco de Miranda, who was going to Bogotá, on a "Newspaper-editing expedition." Bentham also sent by Miranda a letter of introduction to Simón Bolívar. In this letter Bentham, evidently unaware of the details of Francisco de Miranda's capture, stated, "His name will of course suffice to ensure, at your hands, all such kind attentions as his disposition and acquirements may show that he is qualified for receiving." Again Bentham stressed the value and power of the press. "The function he is gone to exercise, or at least to endeavour to exercise, under the protection of your laws I mean that of the Editor of a newspaper is one, especially in a rising country such as yours, to the importance of which you cannot but be fully sensible."[25]

Bentham's final comment on liberty of the press in Spanish America appeared in a letter to José del Valle. The Central American had on May 19, 1829, written Bentham a letter about a nation's coins, asking him what he thought should appear on them. Bentham chided his correspondent for thus spending his effort when it "might have been employed in the production of effects, in which contribution to public happiness had been more determinate and unquestionable." After mentioning two political items, he turned to liberty of the press and gently led del Valle through his reasoning on the subject. He added little if anything to his earlier statements, but he gave a convincing argument in its favor. Periodicals, he claimed, are the "principally effective literary instruments of good and evil" with the daily newspaper being the most. If a nation had only a government daily newspaper, even with an honest editor, bad effects would result. For, Bentham argued, he would either bend to the desire of the constitutional au-

24. Hall to Bentham, October 17, 1822, in UCL, XII, 85; Hall to William Empson, November 2, 1823, in UCL, XII, 133.
25. Hall to Bentham, October 17, 1822, in UCL, XII, 91; Bentham to Bolívar, January 6, 1823, in UCL, XII, 86.

thorities or, if he remained honest, he would have given the public only his own nothings. To minimize this evil, Bentham suggested his plan for assuring the publication of political criticism from various correspondents (communicators). "If matters can be so ordered that he shall stand bound to give place to observations in equal quantity made in opposition to his own, or those of any other writer upon the side which he advocates, this [is] as much as can be done."

Then, he told del Valle that "when Miranda, son of the celebrated General Miranda, with whom I was on intimate terms, went some years ago from this country, in which he was born and bred to Colombia—to set up a newspaper in the English style, I drew up for his use a little plan, having for its object this species of impartiality and independence, as far as practicable." He promised to send a copy of this to del Valle if he could find it. But in the meantime, he suggested that del Valle give some consideration to solving the problem of freedom of the press in his own country.[26]

Did Bentham draw up a new plan for Leander Miranda? His papers do not reveal it. Or did he simply give him a copy of what he had prepared for Leander's father over a decade before?

26. Bentham to del Valle, May 19, 1829, in Add. MSS 33546, BM.

Six

JUNCTIANA CANAL

WHILE BENTHAM PLANNED, schemed, worked for the establishment of a New World utilitarian utopia, he admitted in one major instance that such an achievement was not yet reality: the area was not sufficiently developed to take on the major task of the construction of an interoceanic canal. Spanish America here needed the assistance of its near neighbor, the Anglo-American United States. In 1822, Bentham devised a plan for a canal which is remarkable in its solution to the problems inherent in such an undertaking and in its similarity to what eventually happened with the building of the Panama Canal.

A water passage to connect the Atlantic and Pacific Oceans became a passionate desire of Spain "from the year 1513 in which Núñez de Balboa discovered the Pacific Ocean."[1] When the search for a natural water route failed, Spain decided to build a canal. In 1528 Spain proposed to cut four canals through Middle America: from the Lake of Nicaragua to the South Sea, from the River Chagres to Panama, across the Isthmus of Tecuantepec, and from Nombre de Dios to Panama. In 1800 she added two more possible canal sites to her list: from Rio Grande near Panama to Rio Chagres and from Rio Caymito to the Embarcadero of Rio Trini-

---

1. A version of this chapter appeared in *The Americas: A Quarterly Review of Inter-American Cultural History*, XXVII, July, 1970. Napoleon Garella, engineer-in-chief, Royal Corps of Miners of France, 1842, as quoted in Miles P. Duval, Jr., *Cadiz to Cathay* (Palo Alto, California, 1947), 1.

dad.[2] But none of Spain's plans came to fruition, and independence came to Spanish America without the construction of an interoceanic canal.

The creation of a water passage remained of vital interest, however, to many nations, in particular to the United States, England, and France. As this rivalry was developing, Bentham wrote his plan. The manuscript for this proposal is in his amanuensis' handwriting with some marginal notes in Bentham's own hand. A title page, probably a second copy, dated "1823 Nov. 18" and titled "Junctiana Proposal as June 20 to 24 1822" is in Bentham's handwriting."[3]

Bentham proposed the building of a Nicaraguan canal on land ceded by Mexico, with Mexico[4] to be its northern neighbor and Colombia its southern. A joint-stock company financed largely by British investors would build the canal, to be called Junctiana.[5] This new state created by the Mexican land grant through which the canal would be built was to become a part of what Bentham termed "The Anglo-American United States."

The company would build a canal at the Nicaragua site to link the Atlantic Ocean to the San Juan River, thence to Lake Nicaragua and on to the Pacific by way of a river to Lake León or by a shorter, more direct cut. Bentham enumerated the advantages of this route over others, such as the "dead level" elevation of the land between the oceans, the great depths of the various bodies of water, and the small size of the cuts necessary to bring them together. Bentham supported his choice of site by writing, "Neither in Humboldt's work, nor in any other as yet published, is any considerable part of the above information (it is believed) to be found. Under these circumstances the Nicaragua track seems to be the one, the only one, to which, in the present state of our knowledge

2. As shown on map by Aaron Arrowsmith, published June 1, 1803, in London as it appears in A. Arrowsmith, *Atlas to Thompson's Alcedo: Dictionary of America and West Indies* (London, 1816), plate XIII.

3. "Junctiana Proposal as June 20 to 24 1822," in UCL, CVI, 266–67.

4. Mexico at this time included all of New Spain, that is, Central America and Mexico.

5. Bentham used the terms Junctiana and Junctiania interchangeably.

here in Europe, the attention of capitalists can be directed, with a view to the formation of any such company as is here proposed."[6]

Using Pinkerton's *Atlas*, Bentham proposed that Junctiania extend from the mouth of the San Juan River in the Atlantic to the mouth of the León River in the Pacific, covering in breadth about sixty miles. The boundaries of the new state were to be a chain of lofty mountains in the north; in the south, another chain of mountains except for the "dead level" area; to the east, the Atlantic; to the west, partly mountains, with Costa Rica on one side and the Pacific Ocean on the other.

The company would gain revenue from the price of transit which all ships using the waterway would pay, and from the land itself which the company would sell, lease, build on or use in any other way. The obligations of the company were to pay the local authorities "a sum in the name of purchase money for the powers of government," to pay indemnification due to all individuals including the Indians who had previously owned the land (but at present value only), and to pay for the building and operation of the canal and the necessary fortifications. But, here for the first of many times, Bentham stated flatly that the price of transit must be the same for all nations.

While the company would at all times demand the right to the price of transit and the rents and profits of its lands, Bentham did not believe that it could adequately function as a government. He predicted that it would constantly use its right of patronage and would go from "worse to worse." Nor could Mexico and Colombia provide the security necessary to protect the major investments of the company because "states so lately emancipated from so bad a form of government, can not but appear to stand exposed; society and manners, on the part of so large a portion of the population being as yet on so unfavorable a footing."[7]

Bentham believed that such a situation demanded "the establishment of a form of government, which has for its object the greatest happiness of the greatest number of people." But the

6. "Junctiana Proposal," 1822, in UCL, CVI, 266–67.
7. *Ibid.*, 268–70.

people of that area of Mexico were "not as yet of sufficient age to go alone." This utilitarian utopia could not be found in either Colombia or Mexico, but only in the United States. "Well then, in Washington may be seen an institution, which has long been in the habit of taking an infant state to nurse. Witness Indiana, Illinois, Alabama, Missouri: and how excellent the system of nursing is—how admirable a dry nurse the President has always been— experience has abundantly testified." Bentham pointed out that the United States in the beginning would be "in the state of the hen with one chick. But out of so fertile a womb, say who can, how many more such chicks may not be destined to be poured forth." With this one comment, Bentham ceased discussing such expansionist ideas.[8] However, in spite of his evident admiration for the United States, Bentham was aware of the controversy brewing over slavery as the United States began to expand: "No slavery, in any shape, to be allowed. Should any vessel, with any slaves on board, obtain admittance into the territory, every such slave, upon his entrance within the territory, is to be free."[9]

The company itself would build fortifications for the canal which it would maintain and control, but in case of aggression by sea, the very existence of the United States Navy should remove the smallest danger of attack from other states. Indeed, why should a nation attack Junctiana? To destroy it would be to hurt oneself; and to take it and keep it would require an army and navy large enough to defeat the United States, Colombia, and Mexico. Not only would the United States guarantee Junctiania from such outside aggression, it would also provide domestic tranquillity by preventing misconduct on the part of the inhabitants toward the company.

The United States was to benefit most from the water communication. Bentham accurately foresaw the commercial growth of the United States. "Erelong, in the natural course of things, it [the United States commercial navy] cannot fail of being superior even to that of England." He envisioned United States growth in the

8. *Ibid.*, 291, 285.
9. *Ibid.*, 270.

Pacific enhanced by the speedier water communication and predicted that great glory would come to the United States for its Junctiania role—"glory not of that bloody hue which (it is hoped) is growing more and more out of fashion . . . the glory radiating from the uncontrovertible proof that will thus be given, of its having been looked up to as the nation which, in the opinion of two other free nations, stands highest in the composite scale of national probity, wisdom and benevolence."[10]

Since Mexico was to give the land for the canal, Bentham concentrated in his proposal on convincing Mexico of the merit and validity of his plan. He began by urging that Mexico not try to build a canal alone because of incurring the wrath of Colombia since "many months ago, a competent person was sent out from Europe by Colombia to make surveys" for building a canal. Thus a purely Mexican canal would anger Colombia. Bentham admitted that this was his idea for which he was alone answerable since he knew none of the individuals who would be involved in such an undertaking, but "the propensities so universal in human nature constitute the only source, from whence these indications of probable hostility have been derived." Bentham remained convinced, however, that the completion of the waterway according to his plan would bring a state of cordial and durable amity to Mexico and Colombia, and the infant state Junctiania would view them as common parents. Should any misunderstanding arise, the United States would act as a common friend and common reference because "for impartiality, probity and sound sense [the United States] has assuredly never as yet been matched in the history of nations."[11]

If Mexico determined to build the canal alone, she could scarcely hope to do so without foreign capital. The project would require several million pounds sterling and would be years in producing returns on the investment. Bentham questioned Mexico's ability to finance it through taxes or through investments by Mexican citizens. He felt that there was not sufficient wealth in the

10. *Ibid.*, 295–96.
11. *Ibid.*, 272, 279.

hands of Mexicans that individuals would choose to invest funds in such a long-range project when 15 percent and more could be gained on other Mexican investments. Yet English capitalists would rush to invest their money, as they had shown when they invested in the London Docks, which had expected a maximum 10 percent yield.

If Mexico had to resort to foreign capital in addition to native, "then comes the question about the portion of the *territory*, and the *cession* to be made of it." If only the area actually needed for the waterway be ceded, then Mexico had no problem since her territory would still surround Junctiania. If the waterway should be entirely within the Mexican state, however, Mexico lacked the strength at sea to adequately defend it. The canal itself might become "a bone of contention to all nations." And in any war "the most prominent object would of course be this matchless jewel— this matchless key to commercial advantage: the first endeavor would be—either to take possession of it, or to destroy it (as England did by the Washington Capitol): and, in either case, what would be the condition of the Company?" But Bentham's proposal had as its direct object:

Securing the establishment of the communication for the benefit of all nations without exceptions: and more particularly for the benefit of Mexico, Columbia, and the Anglo-American States; these being the three nations to which local proximity will render it in a peculiar degree advantageous. But moreover for its *collateral* object, it has the prevention of all that ill will as between Mexico and Columbia. . . . This heart-burning, this source of war and disappointment—this it is, that presents itself to view as the great natural *stumbling block* to the undertaking: this stumbling block, it is the principal object of this proposal to remove.[12]

Should Mexico agree to his proposed cession, Bentham refused to suggest whether Mexico should be paid, and, if so by whom, Colombia, the company, or the two together. Instead he maintained that these questions "of necessity, must, in the present

12. *Ibid.*, 274–77.

stage of business, be left unanswered." He could not, however, re-
strain himself from saying that should Mexico demand a price for
the cession there would be no glory to Mexico, and embarrassment
and obstruction would begin because of the inability of finding
suitable grounds for valuation. No one would be satisfied with any
possible settlement. One cardinal principle must be consistently
observed, no matter what Mexico's final decision was. Again Bentham repeated, "No *preference* must there be, in respect of the *price
of transit.*" If such was allowed, the simplicity and merit of the
plan would be consequently destroyed.

As an incentive to agreement common to both Mexico and Colombia alike, Bentham pointed out the immediate creation of a
new and prosperous state, Junctiania, with its two towns, one on
the Atlantic and the other on the Pacific which "would present to
every eye the civilized world in miniature." Added in Bentham's
own handwriting is a brief description of the types of people who
would come: "The functionaries of the superintending classes . . .
the members of the establishment, civil and military . . . would
form a sensible addition to the active population and circulating
wealth of the territory even from the very commencement of the
work."[13]

Soon this mass of wealth and population would begin to run
over and "spread itself over the two great states on each side of it."
This particular advantage no other state could share in the least.
In addition Mexico and Colombia would find in Junctiania "a
Common School, established under the eyes of both of them, an
all comprehensive School, of every thing that is useful in art and
science, but more particularly of those things that are most useful,
good legislation, good judicature, good government in every line.
This indeed supposes and assumes, that the territory of Junctiania
will be a member of the Anglo-American United States, and
thereby, that the government will be in the only form, to which
that School can give admittance."[14]

As for the rest of the world, all nations would gain from the

13. *Ibid.*, 281, 283.
14. *Ibid.*, 284.

existence of an interoceanic waterway without losing anything. At this point Bentham ended his Junctiania proposal. It is conceivable that this was simply the preface or even prospectus to a longer, more detailed plan; for a note on the manuscript dated "1822 June 24," folio 106, page 297 states, "So much sent to Mr. Barrio, November 26, 1823."

It is difficult to determine when Bentham began to develop his canal project. He referred to it at length in a long letter to Bernardino Rivadavia, minister of state for Buenos Aires, dated the thirteenth of June, 1822. He told Rivadavia that in a recent letter to Bolívar he had suggested his Junctiana plan. Bentham could not remember if he had talked with Bolívar about this before, but he reported to Rivadavia that upon mentioning the possibility of an interoceanic canal to Bolívar's agent, Echeverría, he learned that the Colombian government was already considering this and that an engineer had been sent out in February of that year to make surveys for the project. Echeverría told Bentham that Colombia hoped to be able to finance the project alone, and would seek foreign capital only if that proved impossible. Bentham related all this to Rivadavia, remarking that Echeverría had expressed no desire for secrecy. He continued in his letter to describe in broad outline the plan he wrote within the next two weeks as the Junctiana proposal.[15]

Bentham used a single source for the basic geographical parts of his plan. It was perhaps this one book, William Davis Robinson's *Memoirs of the Mexican Revolution*, that prompted him to write out his own solution to the canal problem. Bentham did not pretend to have used any source other than Robinson in his choice of site. Yet he evidently misread or only partially read this book, for Robinson actually proposed two sites:

Having thus attempted to elucidate the extraordinary and peculiar advantages which Costa Rica possesses for the establishment of a navigable intercourse between the two seas, we will now proceed to examine another position, which, although it is deficient in some of the natural ad-

15. Bentham to Rivadavia, June 13, 1822, in UCL, LX, 16–19. A partial copy of this letter is also found in XII, 387–88.

vantages of Costa Rica, still possesses others of so important a character as to render it almost doubtful with us at which of the two places the desired communication ought first to be opened. Were we to consult the present and future interests of Mexico, and of the republic of the United States, we should say that the Mexican Isthmus (or as it is more properly designated, the Isthmus of Tehuantepec) is the section before all others on the American continent, where the communication between the Pacific and Atlantic Oceans should be made.[16]

But Bentham makes no mention of this part of Robinson's work and concentrated on the Nicaragua route for his plan.

Bentham used much the same documentation that Robinson had used, evidently without checking it. Both Robinson and Bentham remarked that William Pitt was particularly enthusiastic about the construction of such a canal, and Bentham stated that General Francisco Miranda, under the protection of Pitt, contemplated such an enterprise. Both Bentham and Robinson referred to an article about a New World canal that appeared in the *Edinburgh Review* in 1810. But the article from which Robinson quoted actually appeared in the *Review* for October 1808–January 1809 and was entitled "Lettre aux Espanols Americains. Par un de leur Compatriotes. A Philadelphie." Written by James Mill assisted by General Miranda, it is a brief review of the efforts made for the independence of Spanish America in both England and Spanish America itself. The author enumerated the advantages of independence, pointing out the commercial opportunities of an interoceanic canal at either Panama or Nicaragua. This canal discussion, however, involved only about two pages of a thirty-five page article.[17] The article was hardly a definitive study of the canal, and it does not substantiate the impression Bentham gave in his plan that "it was from Miranda that the *Edinburgh Review* derived the

16. William Davis Robinson, *Memoirs of the Mexican Revolution* (2 vols., London, 1821), II, 285. Robinson generally refers to the Nicaragua route as being in Costa Rica, but states, "The province of Costa Rica or, as it is named by some geographers, Nicaragua" (II, 276).

17. *Edinburgh Review or Critical Journal* for October 1808–January 1809, XIII, 277–311.

principal part of the information contained in its article on the subject in 1810."[18]

Yet Bentham needed only the bare essentials of an idea from any source. His purpose was to design not an engineering plan but a political and economic project within feasible engineering limits which could function as a vehicle for implementing his own ideas. Here utilitarianism was to reign supreme from the beginning.

In little more than a year after Bentham finished drafting his Junctiana proposal, it was outdated. On July 1, 1823, Central America ceased to be a part of Mexico, and Bentham's grand design for the creation of a member of the United States between Gran Colombia and the Mexican empire was now impossible. This did not deter Bentham, however, in his efforts to see his plan fulfilled. Without making any changes in the Junctiana proposal, he sent a copy of it to a Guatemalan who was in England at that time, José María del Barrio. Prior to this time Bentham had agreed to help del Barrio come to the attention of Foreign Secretary George Canning. Bentham's papers at University College Library contain two letters in Bentham's hand, one dated "1823 Nov. 19" with the heading "From Del Barrio to Sec'y Canning First Draught not employed," the second, "From Del Barrio to Sec'y Canning—Second Draught not employed" dated the following day. Whether Bentham actually sent a letter to Canning from del Barrio is unknown.

In the two drafts of this letter that Bentham wrote for del Barrio, he identified del Barrio as of noble birth,[19] as a delegate to the late Spanish Cortes, and soon to be special agent of Guatemala in Europe. The purpose of Bentham's letter for del Barrio was twofold: to get British recognition of the new state and to get support and approval for an interoceanic canal.

Bentham's project for a canal was not mentioned by name in either of the drafts of del Barrio's letters to Canning. The threat of

18. "Junctiana Proposal," 1822, in UCL, CVI, 265.
19. Bentham to Secretary George Canning, November 9, 10, 1823, in UCL, LX, 75–85. In del Barrio's memorandum to Bentham, he told Bentham that his was the first family in Guatemala and the only title in Guatemala belonged to his second cousin, a marquis, and that many of both his maternal and paternal relatives in Spain were titled.

French involvement in the building of a canal was broadly hinted at with the promise of details to be furnished in a private interview. The site was already chosen, Bentham's choice, of course: "Lake Nicaragua (it is sufficiently established) affords a most promising spot for the junction, and far superior to every other. Baron Humboldt . . . is satisfied of this." The two things necessary for this project were capital and auxiliary defense. Capital would be sought from England, aid for defense from the United States. For the outlay of capital, del Barrio's country would give up as private property whatever area was necessary for joint direction, with the single stipulation of an equality of tolls and the prevention of excessive tolls. Then England, being a maritime nation, would gain most from equal tolls. So in essence del Barrio presented the Bentham plan. Del Barrio further assured the secretary that he had not yet started taking subscriptions for such a project.

It is difficult to determine how interested del Barrio was in Bentham's project. Surely he was interested in British recognition, and perhaps the canal project was the price he had to pay for Bentham's assistance in providing an entrée to Canning. The only correspondence from del Barrio in the University College collection is an undated memorandum to Bentham. In it del Barrio told Bentham that he had visited the proposed canal site in 1818 and in a one line postscript he added, "The first person I shall see in Paris is Humboldt."[20]

What happened to the plan for this meeting of Canning and del Barrio? What happened to del Barrio or to Bentham's interest in his canal project? In Rafael Heliodoro Valle's collection, *Cartas de José Cecilio del Valle, capítulo X*, is a series of letters to and from José María del Barrio in the years 1827–1831. At this time del Barrio was in Mexico and the two Guatemalans discussed Mexican, Central American, and Guatemalan politics, literature, and philosophy as well as mundane bits of gossip. In a letter dated "Mejico

20. *Ibid.*, 75–85. Bentham had wanted del Barrio to ask for an interview, but del Barrio insisted that he simply let Secretary Canning know that he was available should Canning wish to see him. He further informed Bentham that he was leaving the next morning for Paris, where he would inform the British Embassy of his address.

Mayo 16 de 1827," del Barrio described Bentham's house and ideas, and his own custom of eating with Bentham once or twice each week. In other letters Bentham and his works were mentioned, but not a word about the canal.[21]

An interesting Bentham document dated November 20, 1823, the same day as the second letter that Bentham drafted for del Barrio to Canning, advocated that Spain build a canal in Nicaragua. The proposal, written in French in an amanuensis' hand, stressed the value of a canal in developing Central America as an entrepot of the world, as an agricultural region, as a source of "Corvina" fish (which could perhaps replace the cod), and as a means of countering and reducing the growing strength of great Britain there, as well as creating a shorter passage to Asia. Much of the document reads as though it were copied from a geography text, and indeed, many paragraphs are followed by page numbers; yet parts of the document are unmistakably Bentham. Absent, however, are the demand for equality of tolls and other characteristic utilitarian principles. As a postscript to the document Bentham stated that he had hardly finished this memorandum when the Spanish ambassador informed him that the Spanish court had knowledge of his plan, but circumstances did not permit the court to concern itself with it at that time. On the final page, which strangely enough is dated "1823 Nov. 19," Bentham revealed his disgust with such an outcome. "J'ai passé ma vie dans l'étude et les travaux de la politique avec les premiéres tetes de corps diplomatique de l'Europe: je n'en ai retiré aucune utilité pour ma fortune."[22]

21. José Cecilio del Valle, *Cartas de José Cecilio del Valle* (Tegucigalpa, Honduras, 1963), 203.

22. "Junctiana Proposal," 1822, in UCL, CVI, 298–306.

Seven

EDUCATION

EDUCATION OF THE PEOPLE, with its forming of the public mind, became an ancillary concern of Bentham because it was vital to the success of his ideas, particularly in Spanish America where education was thin and scattered and the public mind a mere shadow. One of his first Spanish American documents, "Intended for Caracas on the occasion of General Miranda's expedition," began with a recommendation of the use of the Lancaster method. After this, however, Bentham did not urge Spanish America to follow a particular educational formula. This was in contrast to his persistent recommendations concerning the adoption and use of his code and the means of creating stable republican governments. Bentham's later Spanish American documents reflect much more specific educational concerns, such as the proper choice of books and the advantages of Hazelwood School, an experimental institution that pioneered in student government.

Bentham was not alone in seeing the possibilities in the Lancaster system of teaching for Spanish America. Several Mexican deputies to the Spanish Cortes sponsored bills supporting it, and, with the coming of independence, the method became widely used throughout Spanish America.[1] It had been developed almost simultaneously in England by Joseph Lancaster and Andrew Bell and provided for a system of monitors, that is older students who

1. Jaime Rodríguez, *The Emergence of Spanish America* (Berkeley, 1975), 57.

taught the younger students. This plan for mutual instruction was designed to educate the poor inexpensively. Bentham in his statement for Caracas wondered if someone from Venezuela should come to England to learn the method or whether someone from England should go there to teach it, or both. Bentham suggested to Miranda that soon literacy might become a prerequisite for marriage as well as for voting and that the Lancaster method could provide this for the working classes. This requirement would ensure that each person entering the marital state would have knowledge of his or her obligations and rights. It was to be hoped that this might prevent some improvident marriage contracts, and it could also provide the stimulus by which a young person could be urged to learn to read and write.[2]

In this initial document, Bentham recommended, in addition to the Lancaster method, the creation of a school of arts where the useful arts might also be taught to the children of the poor. Whether he thought this school should use mutual teaching techniques is not clear; however, he is explicit about the physical plant. Bentham, opting for the concrete achievement, recommended for this school a building in the shape of his panopticon. This he called a "Panopticon polychreston" with a central hall that would serve not only as a school but also a church, a court, a concert hall, and an assembly room which could be used for political meetings. The adjoining spaces might be used as a school, a hospital, a prison, or a combination of all. Curtains could be used to cut off areas when concerts were given, and if it were used as a prison, church services could be held without the necessity of moving prisoners to another building or room. Immediately following the suggestion of a panopticon building, Bentham sug-

---

2. Bentham to Bolívar, September 27, 1822, in UCL, XII, 88. The trustees of the Royal Lancastrian Society appended to "Report of Joseph Lancaster's Progress from 1798," published in 1810, comments which reported that "a deputation from Caracas had come to England expressly to see the working of the school and that the government of that country had since sent two young men to the Borough Road to learn the system." *Dictionary of National Biography*, XI, 481. This same source stated that Bolívar himself had visited that school in 1810 and in 1825 received Joseph Lancaster with due consideration in Caracas.

gested, "A Draught for this purpose may probably be had from
. . . J. Bentham."[3]

Although Bentham had been rather open in his attacks on the
Church of England, he was, for the most part, very circumspect in
dealing with matters of religion in his Spanish American documents. But Bentham endeavored to use every available resource
in carrying out his plans. So, aware of the role of the Church and
the power of the parish priests, he recommended that parish
priests be required to take courses to increase their usefulness. He
suggested that as soon as courses in natural history, philosophy,
and medical sciences were established, attendance might be required of all parish priests as well as those who hoped to someday
serve in that capacity. The reasons for this requirement, as Bentham saw it, were two: to serve "as an antidote to those mischievous superstitions, with which the minds of that order of man are
so liable to be infected," and to enable them where professional
assistance was unavailable to help their parishioners with needed
advice and assistance, particularly in the medical field. He had
great faith in such a plan, explaining that "none can be so stupid
and inept" as not to retain some of such "salutary" information,
while the more intelligent could become correspondents of any
academy of science when it was established. If nothing else, the
parish priests could keep the public aware of current happenings
by acting as "commodious *Channels of Communication*" through
which the government might inform the people of laws passed,
decisions made, *etc*. This could be accomplished by the "Government publishing a weekly or other periodical newspaper, the contents of it might be read to the Congregation by the Parish Priest
immediately before or after divine service."[4]

Between the time of this statement for Venezuela, 1810, and his
next Spanish American document, 1818, Bentham, probably because of the interest and influence of James Mill and other friends,
drew up his own plan for the proper education of the growing English middle class. He applied the principles of Lancaster and Bell

3. "Caracas Necessity of an all Comprehensive Code," 1810, in UCL, XII, 88.
4. *Ibid.*

to secondary teaching, creating in the end his *Chrestomathia*, which he published in 1816–1817. As one would expect, the plan is highly systematized, and every detail is elaborately worked out. Bentham emphasized the great need and value of charts, diagrams, specimens, models, *etc.* Each child was to be carefully examined to be sure that he understood the concepts and had not simply learned by rote.[5] He stressed science and minimized Latin and Greek. He was so excited about his plan that he offered his garden to Francis Place and others so that they might open such a school.[6] Place, a staunch Benthamite, is best known as the author of the People's Charter (Chartist Movement), which drew heavily from Bentham's ideas. A larger school on this order was to be set up at Leicester Square on property to be purchased by David Ricardo. Ricardo, who had been instructed by James Mill, developed with others of the Manchester School the doctrine of laissez faire, which is still referred to as classical economics. The project was abandoned, however, when the shop keepers of the area opposed it, probably because of its insistence on the exclusion of religion.[7]

Although the Chrestomathia school did not come into full existence, a school was established that met Bentham's standards. This was the Hazelwood School at Birmingham operated by Rowland Hill. Bentham was delighted with the school when he read the report of Hill's eldest brother, Matthew Davenport Hill: *Plans for the Government and Liberal Instructions of Boys in large Numbers, drawn from Experience*,[8] published in London in 1823. As Bentham described it to Bolívar, "I can give you no better proof than by saying that upon looking into the book, in which this just product of genius and long experience is brought to view in detail I gave up with the utmost satisfaction a plan of my own which had occupied no small part of my time, and to which I had determined to sacrifice the greatest part of that garden, your visit to which will be a matter of record: a plan for which I was on the point of

5. Brian Simon, *Studies in the History of Education, 1780–1870* (London, 1960), 79–82.

6. *Dictionary of National Biography*, II, 274.

7. Simon, *Studies in the History of Education*, 82.

8. For an interesting review of the book see the article by Basil Hall in *Edinburgh Review*, XL (January, 1825), 315–35.

putting to hazard some thousands of my moderate property."[9] An accounts book of Bentham for 1822–1825 reveals that Bentham sent various parts of his Chrestomathic plan to Spanish America, but in his letters to leaders there he did not discuss his own plan. Instead he recommended Hazelwood School, where a form of student government allowed the students to have practice in the arts of legislation and judicial decision. This, added to the fact that Hazelwood followed to a great degree Bentham's own ideas as pronounced in *Chrestomathia*, increased his enthusiasm for Hill's school.[10]

Bentham wrote in detail of Hazelwood to Simón Bolívar, but he evidently also recommended it quite highly to Bernardino Rivadavia of Buenos Aires. In the printed *Supplement to the Codification Proposal. Part II. Testimonials* Bentham included a letter from Rivadavia, dated August 26, 1822, in praise of Bentham and his work, along with a rather extraneous footnote regarding Hazelwood. The footnote reads in its entirety:

At the recommendation of Mr. Bentham, Mr. Rivadavia sent two of his sons to Messrs. Hill's school at Hazelwood, near Birmingham, from which an off-set is just planted at Bruce Castle, near Tottenham, and so well satisfied has Mr. Rivadavia been with the situation of these his sons, that six more pupils have come from that part of late Spanish America, making, in the whole, eight, among whom some are relations of Mr. Rivadavia. Editor[11]

Bentham, in his attempts to persuade Bolívar to similar action, informed him of Rivadavia's action.[12]

9. "Caracas Necessity," 1810, in UCL, XII, 88.

10. On November 8, 1823, Bentham sent his *Chrestomathia* to José del Barrio of Guatemala; Leander Miranda on December 9, 1822, was given *Chrestomathia*, parts 1 and 2 and on December 11, 1822, was given two copies of the Chrestomathia Table. On June 6, 1822, José Echeverría was given six copies of the Chrestomathia Table for the constituted authorities at Bogotá. On June 27, 1822, Miguel Digne Estrada of Mexico was given copies of *Chrestomathia*, parts 1 and 2. Add MSS 33563, BM. The Chrestomathia Table was Bentham's specific design of the curriculum for his school for the middle and upper classes. Laden with words of his own creation that were never accepted, the Table is heavily weighted in favor of science and vocational training.

11. Jeremy Bentham, *Supplement to the Codification Proposal. Part II* (London, n.d.), 99.

12. Bentham to Bolívar, January 6, 1823, in UCL, XII, 343.

The letter to Bolívar that carried such an unqualified endorse-
ment, or, as Bentham put it, "Eulogium," of Hazelwood was a recommendation to the Liberator of the son of Bolívar's old leader
Francisco de Miranda. Bentham assured Bolívar that he would
have sent young Leander to Hazelwood "had he fallen in my way
a few years earlier." There he could have learned not only lan-
guages but the useful branches of art and science, and most especially, "he would then have learnt, not only in theory, but even
from practice, though on such a miniature scale, the arts of legislation and judicature, taught, in conjunction with private morality in the most delightful as well as efficiently instructive manner imaginable." This early form of student government evidently
appealed greatly to Bentham.[13]

Leander Miranda, Bentham wrote to Bolívar, had taken with
him a copy of the first edition of Hill's book about Hazelwood.
Bentham sent the second edition to Bolívar, reiterating the impact that Hill's work had had on his own educational endeavors.
Hill had added to the intellectual emphasis a moral branch which
Bentham described as having resulted from "genius operating
upon experience which had never been within my past." Thus Bentham became Hill's champion and boasted to Bolívar that Hill reported that he, Bentham, had been the means of doubling the en-
rollment at Hazelwood.[14]

Bentham recommended to Bolívar that his government might
send one or two young men to learn the techniques of Hazelwood
so that they might return to Colombia and Peru and open such
schools. If two were sent, then one might return after only a year,
while the other could stay on to gain greater efficiency. Anticipating the dearth of funds available to the government, Bentham suggested that Bolívar might find parents with sufficient funds to
send their sons to England and then, if the sons were competent,
assure them of a position upon their return from Hazelwood. Such
positions should include a salary sufficient for their subsistence
but one largely dependent on the number of scholars enrolled in

13. *Ibid.*, 88.
14. *Ibid.*, 343–44.

their schools. Annual costs for students at Hazelwood Bentham estimated at about £80 a year, exclusive of transportation to and from England. But it would be well worth it. Bentham assured Bolívar that he "would stake upon me any little reputation it may happen me to have" that such boys, assuming they were naturally well qualified, would return to their parents better qualified for conducting affairs of state than the cabinet ministers that England had produced. In addition Bentham volunteered "in the course of the short time I can expect to live" to "keep a guarding eye" on the welfare of any boy Bolívar might want to recommend to Hazelwood.[15]

In the course of his discussion of Hazelwood, Bentham had denounced "the two great public calamities, the Universities of Oxford and Cambridge and home/nest and hotbeds of political corruption in its most odious form." These institutions were so expensive yet so overcrowded that they must "close the door to useful teachings and to the general habits of applications." Then Bentham told Bolívar of the plan of a group of liberals at the cost of some £300,000 sterling to open a university at London which would be open to students of any religious persuasion. (Even so, in Bentham's opinion, as good as this university would be, it would still be inferior to Hazelwood School unless London became in addition a school of legislation and jurisprudence.)[16]

Bolívar did not receive Bentham's letter of August, 1825, until December of 1826. In a copy of a rough draft published in *Cartas del Libertador* Bolívar thanked him for his offer to receive "with benevolence" the boys he might choose to send to Hazelwood. He would like to take advantage of the offer because the school's plan for practical education seemed to him to be "the best of the inventions for developing the human spirit." He lamented the burden of slavery that through the years had destroyed man spiritually and made him almost unworthy of liberty. Thus the cultivation of the sciences of which Bentham spoke in his letter would help man discover his rights. And in Bolívar's forty-year struggle to end

15. *Ibid.*, 344, 88, 343.
16. O'Leary (ed.), *Memorias del General O'Leary*, XII, 274.

oppression to the march of youth, Hazelwood could distinguish itself by its method of facilitating instruction. He closed this subject by assuring Bentham, "Thus I am persuaded by what you have told me of that important institution." Before ending the letter he asked Bentham to send him again the works on national education—probably a reference to Hill's work.[17]

Bentham's concern for education went beyond the establishment of schools or the training of a few boys as headmasters. His faith in the efficacy of the printed word led Bentham to send printed copies and even drafts of his works to virtually all of his Spanish American correspondents. He frequently boasted of the number of copies of his works that had been sold in Spanish America.

Bentham believed that a prerequisite to self-government and stability and, of course, to a state based on utilitarian principles was the shaping of the public mind. Thus he tried to assist the young nations in choosing books—books that would enrich the mind and develop attitudes appropriate for those who now ruled their own destiny. In what appears to be a letter to Bolívar, undated, Bentham speaks of Antonio A. de Jonte, agent for Chile in England, for whom he had prepared a list of French books, especially those in the "moral branch of science, history and politics included, as occasioned to me as best adapted to the purpose of contributing to form the public mind in those two countries," namely Buenos Aires and Chile. Bentham also went to great lengths to locate books for Jonte on diplomacy or "Letters of Conduct," one for the English monarch and one that the president of the United States might use. Finally after Jonte's departure Bentham managed to obtain these works, which he dispatched to Chile.[18]

17. Lecuna (ed.), *Cartas del Libertador*, VI, 154–55.
18. Bentham to Bolívar (?), undated, in UCL, X, 3–4. In a letter from Bentham to Rivadavia dated February 20, 1819, Bentham tells Rivadavia that he has been able to get the book on the United States from the United States ambassador, "their worthy Representative," and the other from an English friend, a former ambassador who in addition gave him a copy of his instructions. Bentham was sending copies to Rivadavia and if possible "to your natural ally, Bolívar." Add. MSS 33545, BM.

Bentham's major efforts in choosing proper books came late in his life when he saw a list of books sent by José del Valle. When del Valle's cousin, Prospero de Herrera, went to London in an attempt to get English capital to exploit the family mines, del Valle gave him a list of books which he hoped he could locate and send to him. Herrera gained entrance to the Hermitage, Bentham's home at Queen Square Place, where he asked Bentham's advice concerning the list. These books were intended for the private library of del Valle, but when Bentham saw the list, he immediately decided that there must be a greater reason for wanting such books. He asked Herrera "if the books were for enriching the congressional library." Herrera, not wishing to hurt his chances for getting Bentham's advice, replied that Valle "could use them for that purpose."[19]

Bentham evidently did not think the list appropriate or complete. Of the forty-eight listed, Bentham questioned either the existence or value of twenty-one of the titles, beside which he placed a "qy" for query. In a letter concerning this list he commented, "In it I see along with . . . works of the Old School, some very voluminous ones which neither I nor my nephew who is . . . extensively conversant with books ever heard of. On enquiry of Herrera, I find, as I suspected that the selection was made—not in consequence of any recommendation received from any person known to the proposed purchaser but from some list which at Mexico I believe had come into his hands." Here Bentham revealed his thoughts about the significance of books as he concludes, "For an infant State in which Books are in a manner unknown, choice of Books is a branch of legislation."[20]

Bentham then set about to draw up his own list for purchase by del Valle. His papers at University College, London, contain two separate lists, one dated and one not. The list dated "1827

19. Próspero de Herrera to José del Valle, September 15 (no year), in del Valle Papers, as quoted in Louis E. Bumgartner, *José del Valle of Central America* (Durham, N.C., 1963), 259. Bumgartner suggests that "Próspero might have answered in the words of G. A. Thompson that they were only for Valle's 'inordinate requisitions at the feast of the intellect.'"

20. Bentham to Jean Baptiste Say, January 18, 1827, in UCL, XII, 374.

Janvier 15" carries at the top of the sheet in French, "Works in French that Mr. Bentham takes the liberty of recommending to Mr. Herrera for the account of M. del Valle." It contains fifty-six titles covering various fields. The undated one, which looks as though it was not completed, divides the books as follows: legislation with the works of Bentham translated by Dumont first, followed by twelve additional titles; history with twenty-two titles; science with fourteen titles; literature with three; education with two and metaphysics with only one.

Bentham's choices are interesting. His legislative section includes Destutt de Tracy, Montesquieu, and Bernard Fontenelle, as well as collections of constitutions, works on civil, criminal, and procedural codes of England and France, and a penal code for Louisiana. In the field of history he chose Fontenelle's *Memoirs of Madame de Maintenon* (which Voltaire had criticized along with the recent memoirs of that lady by her lady-in-waiting), Jean Charles Sismondi's histories of France and the Middle Ages, Augustín Thierry's *History of the Norman Conquest*, a history of Italy (in a French translation if available), *The Private Life of Louis XV*, and Frances Wright's *View of Society and Manners in the United States* (in a French translation if available). The science section included works on chemistry, anatomy, physics, botany, zoology, and natural history; literature included the *Revue Encyclopedie*, Voltaire and Felix Bodin; metaphysics contained only the single work of Abbé de Condillac that Bentham thought worthy. Interestingly, the two works in the field of education that Bentham recommended are Fénelon's story of Telemachus and those of Pestalozzi, the Swiss educational reformer.[21] *Télémaque*, according to Bowring's biography, played a major role in shaping Bentham's own mind as a child. One might expect to see on this list the works of Lancaster, Bell, or Hill. Perhaps they were not here because they were not in French. Perhaps he had sent copies of these earlier, or perhaps he had forgotten them as he moved on to other endeavors.

21. *Ibid.*, 370, 380.

In the margin of the list with subject divisions is written: "Memorandum Works for Guatemala. This list might be much increased."[22] Bentham, still perceiving del Valle's personal wishes for books as a means of educating and "forming the public mind," moved quickly to do just that on an information sheet entitled "Guatemala" and dated January 7, 1827: "To write to Say, Bodin and Julien to each of them to confer together about the best books in French to form the public mind for the statesmen in Guatemala including arts and sciences, which are cultivated with ardor by Del Valle and to say that I have furnished Herrera with a catalogue of such as I myself have thought of."[23]

On the same sheet appears the note "M. Herrera goes on Friday the 19th at 10 o'clock in the forenoon." On January 18, 1827, he wrote to Jean Baptiste Say, French economist, a letter of introduction of Herrera upon his visit to Paris. This letter carries just under the salutation "Wrote by same conveyance to La Fayette, Julien and Bodin." Bentham enclosed copies in Spanish of letters from del Valle and told them of his request for Bentham's aid in drawing up a code for Guatemala. "He has at the same time commissioned his near relation and confidential agent, Herrera, to purchase a collection of Books which at his own expense he means to employ in forming the commencement of a public library for the formation thereby of the public mind—an operation of which it stands in no small need in particular on the subject of legislation." Here Bentham tells Say of the list del Valle sent, then continues by informing him of the list of books he has drawn up for del Valle "in the character of a proposed substitute to that list, so far as regards French books." Since Bentham felt incompetent to recommend books "in the physical branch in its present state" he asked Say along with Bodin and Julien and any others so disposed to act as a "little Congress of Co-legislators" to add to his list after seeing del Valle's. He assured Say that Herrera would accept "with correspondent gratitude" any assistance they might give. Possibly, too, Dr. Dumont would help in the field of natural his-

22. *Ibid.*, 380.
23. Bentham memorandum, January 7, 1827, in UCL, XXI, 326.

tory. The final paragraph reflects the significance Bentham thought del Valle and his library would have in Guatemala—sufficient for any sacrifice: "I had business enough upon my hands, as you will see, without being loaded with this additional quantity: but the more you know of Del Valle, and of the newborn State, on the destiny of which he is I hope destined to exercise so commanding an influence, the less you will be surprised at the degree of sympathy with which they have inspired one."[24]

In the letter of introduction of Herrera to La Fayette, Bentham apologized for adding to the many people who clamored for the marquis' time, but told him that, since Guatemala was such a young nation he hoped he would receive Herrera. Once more, misconstruing del Valle's plans for the books, he told La Fayette of del Valle's plan to establish a public library at his own expense "for the instruction of his countrymen." While he praised del Valle highly, he did not ask for the marquis' advice in the choice of books.[25]

Bentham's letters bore fruit at least to the extent of Herrera's meeting Bentham's friends in Paris. A letter from Herrera, dated Paris, February 16, 1827, is in the University College collection. This letter, in which Herrera apologized for writing in Spanish, informed Bentham that he had delivered each of the five letters of introduction that Bentham had given him and each in his turn, Bossange, the book dealer, Bodin, La Fayette, Say, and Julien, had received him warmly. Herrera did not mention the books per se, but did comment that he hoped for success before returning to England.[26]

Bentham reported to del Valle in a letter of March 18, 1827, that he had given letters of introduction for his cousin Herrera "to the four men who, I thought, it would be of most use to your country and him that he should be acquainted with." These were, of course, to "la Fayette, so renowned now [by] the whole civilized world," to Julien, the editor of the "most meritorious monthly pub-

24. Bentham to Say, 1827, in UCL, XII, 374.
25. Bentham to Lafayette, January 17, 1827, in UCL, XII, 373.
26. Herrera to Bentham, February 16, 1827, in UCL, XII, 379.

lication in the French language [*Revue Encyclopedie*]—a work that finds its way wherever French is read, John Baptiste Say, the ablest writer on Political Economy in the French language, and Felix Bodin, a principal collaborator on the *Constitutional*—the paper of the most estimable on the liberal side. I have had the satisfaction of being informed by him that he was not dissatisfied with the reception he experienced from any of them." Bentham continued by telling del Valle he had also given Herrera an introduction to Bossange Frères at Paris "with a view to the procurement of Books for your intended library." This book dealer Bentham recommended highly for his "probity and public spirit"[27]

Bentham never recommended books in English to del Valle. He did, however, according to Bowring, send a list of editions of his own works that had appeared in the Peninsula.[28] Bentham realized, perhaps, that while most educated Guatemalans read French as well as Spanish, few knew English.

How many, if any, of these books recommended by Bentham and perhaps some by his friends ever arrived in Guatemala is not revealed in the Bentham papers. But Bentham did send del Valle his works. A letter from Herrera to del Valle dated November 27, 1826 states, "Mr. Bentham . . . has sent to you by Mr. Bowring, a collection of his works."[29] This shipment caused an amusing incident in the Bentham household as revealed by a letter to Bentham from Sarah Austin, who lived with her husband, John, at Queen Square Place and did some translating for Bentham. The letter is dated December 18, 1826.

My dearest Grandpapa,
    As I learn that the books and papers you were so good as to destine for Guatemala are not yet gone, I think it right to tell you what has occurred respecting them within my knowledge since I dined with you.
    Immediately on Mr. Herrera's return to town, which took place within a day or two after I saw you Mr. Prandi communicated to him what you had told me and desired me to tell him,—namely that the packet was

27. Bentham to del Valle, March 18, 1827, in UCL, XII, 382–83.
28. Bowring (ed.), *Works*, XI, 19–20.
29. Del Valle Papers as quoted in Bumgartner, *Jose del Valle of Central America*, 22.

already sent to Guatemala by Mr. Bowring. Mr. Herrera expressed great surprize and regret at this; as he said Del Valle (his cousin) had specially charged him with the negotiation and had sent him and various documents for your inspection which, seeing the turn the thing has taken, he should hardly now feel at liberty to send you.

He afterwards added that he had such strong objections to Mr. Bowring as a mediator, or to that gentleman's having anything to do with the affairs of Guatemala, that he had instantly written to Del Valle to apprize him that the packet was gone—(as he had learned on returning to town) and at the same time to caution him against entering into any correspondence or communication, direct or indirect, with Mr. Bowring.

I have not seen Mr. Herrera; nor had any other communication from him than this—except that he sent me word a few days ago that since the date at which the packet was said to have gone, he, Mr. H. had had three safe and direct means of sending it to the President himself—I should certainly have felt it my duty to make you instantly acquainted with these facts had I not believed the thing to be done and irremediable, and therefore wittingly spared myself the pain of being the medium through which anything in the least degree disagreeable to you, might pass. Now, however, the case wears another aspect & it is not to late to make any change in your determination if you see fit. If not you will, I know, thank me, for telling you facts which may affect your influence in a state where you are so deeply & so justly revered—It is, I believe, unquestionable that Del Valle's influence with *the people* is as unbounded as his zeal for their improvement, & that he will be the most efficient as well as the most willing instrument that you can employ.

But I am going beyond my line here since my only reason for intruding on your attention is the desire that you may know exactly the state of the case and form your *relations* with Guatemala accordingly.[30]

Who finally arranged for the shipment of books remains a mystery, but evidently they were dispatched. Del Valle wrote Bentham on April 18, 1827, "The month of March just passed was one of delightful satisfaction to me. In it I received your letter and your books. They well filled my heart with joy. I recognized the affection which dictated the one, and the kindnesses which remitted the others."[31]

In a letter to Bentham on May 31, 1830, del Valle again thanked

30. Sara Taylor Austin to Bentham, December 18, 1826, in UCL, XII, 358.
31. Del Valle to Bentham, April 18, 1827, in Add. MSS 33546, BM.

him for his letters and books. He lamented the sad condition of Guatemala which needed improvement in virtually every area—agriculture, industry, commerce. "But they are ignorant of the road that would lead to this end, they know not where they ought to commence. They do not possess the economic sciences, nor have they agreed on their cultivation." Then he asked the obvious question, "Submerged for above three centuries in a chaos the most lugubrious, can we expect the sudden production of legislators, statesmen, financiers, etc.?" He then commented on the great increase of public officials "while nothing is thought of that education which is necessary to fit men to fill them . . . there does not exist a single school where the science of legislation is taught . . . no hall in which can be learnt even the elements of good government." He told Bentham of his memorial on education and his hope that "perhaps at last, the voice of reason may be heard."[32]

Bentham evidently gave this letter to Bowring to answer. Bowring responded to del Valle telling him of the many philosophical societies in England, literary, scientific, and agricultural. Bowring then offered himself for membership in the Economic Society of Guatemala so that he might act as a liaison between that body and the many societies in England and elsewhere of which he was a member.[33] Bentham also sent del Valle copies of *Westminster Review* and instructed Bowring to send del Valle, after Bentham's death, future works of his that he had not previously sent.[34]

In what must have been one of del Valle's last letters to Bentham, del Valle responded with words that surely warmed his old friend's heart: "You desire, as I do, universal instruction; and I labour to advance it. There are authorities to whom it is necessary perpetually to refer, in every branch of science—and you are one of them, in every soil I trace your footsteps."[35]

32. Bowring (ed.), *Works*, XI, 49.
.33. Del Valle, *Cartas de José Cecilio del Valle*, 248–49.
34. Bumgartner, *José del Valle of Central America*, 259.
35. Bowring (ed.), *Works*, XI, 71.

Eight

BENTHAM AND HIS
CORRESPONDENTS

BENTHAM, interested in seeing his ideas put into practice, had to depend on local leaders to carry out his ideas when it became evident that he could not immigrate to Spanish America himself. Always an inveterate letter writer, he used his correspondence to guide and direct these leaders. In addition to his comments to them on his major concerns, such as the code, the press, government, and education, there are a number of more mundane topics that should not be overlooked. These provide the shading to Bentham's relationship with that area as they reveal the quality and scope of his interests there. The Spanish Americans—Rivadavia, Bolívar, and del Valle—for their part reacted warmly to Bentham's interest in their work and replied with enthusiasm and flattery.

The Spanish American leader who probably took Bentham most seriously in his endeavors to apply utilitarian philosophy to the creation of a new government was Bernardino Rivadavia of Buenos Aires. In a letter to Simón Bolívar in 1820, Bentham tells of Antonio A. Jonte, agent for Chile in England and a friend of the porteño, "introducing him in 1818 to Rivadavia at that time appointed agent of Buenos Aires to this country, but mostly residing at Paris for the purpose of watching the assemblage of Monarchs and Ministers." Bentham initiated the correspondence with Rivadavia in 1818 and the correspondence between the two continued until April of 1824.[1]

1. Bentham to Bolívar, January 24, 1820, in UCL, X, 3. Three letters to Riva-

As might be expected, Bentham's overriding concern in these letters was that the governments established in Spanish America conform to the greatest happiness principle, and he used his correspondence with Rivadavia to assure this outcome. Such a desire, however, did not move Bentham to engage in long philosophical discussion or in any type of indoctrination of Rivadavia. Instead, he seemed convinced of Rivadavia's adherence to those principles, and he used his letters for other, more pragmatic tasks such as finding suitable assistants for Rivadavia.

Bentham likewise initiated the correspondence between himself and Bolívar. He had had no interest in meeting the Venezuelan in 1810 when he had been in Bentham's own London garden, probably with Francisco de Miranda, visiting James Mill. Bentham told Rivadavia in his letter of February 20, 1819, "I know [Bolívar] by having seen him well in the vicinity of my hermitage, I invisible as usual." And he reminded Bolívar of the occasion in speaking of his garden, "your visit to which will be a matter of record." But as it became more and more evident that the direction of much of Spanish America would be determined by Bolívar, Bentham began the correspondence which lasted for a number of years.[2]

While he felt secure in his own position with Rivadavia, he was less so with Bolívar. Consequently, from the beginning of the correspondence, he seemed particularly concerned that he establish his own reputation as a person of importance. In the first letter,

---

davia and two from him to Bentham are in the Additional Manuscripts of the British Museum. These are dated from 1818 to 1822. The Bentham collection at University College, London, has three letters from Bentham to Rivadavia. The first one, dated in 1818, in French, has inscribed in what appears to be Bentham's hand, "not sent." The other two, one written in 1822, the other in 1824, are in English. Another letter found only in Bowring was written in English.

2. Bentham to Rivadavia, February 20, 1819, in Add. MSS 33545, BM; The UCL collection has six letters from Bentham to Bolívar. The first one, dated January 24, 1820, has a statement at the top questioning whether it had been sent; the second one is dated December 24, 1820; the third, January 6, 1823. The fourth one, June 3, 1823, was evidently dispatched, as was the final one of July 14, 1825. In the UCL collection there is a single letter from Bolívar to Bentham dated September 27, 1822, along with one of the same date to Edward Blaquiere. The *Cartas del Libertador* contains another letter to Bentham, dated January 15, 1827, which is in two parts.

which might not have been posted, he informed Bolívar that Rivadavia had referred to him as "the Newton of legislation," as one destined to become "the legislator of mankind." To emphasize this he said that Dumont reported that an Italian periodical also referred to him as the Newton of legislation. Bentham then turned to the western hemisphere and told Bolívar that Illinois, Alabama, Georgia, and New Hampshire had abolished their laws against usury because of the succinct argument in his "Defense of Usury." Moving then to his own land, he informed Bolívar that Sir Francis Burdett was going to introduce in the House of Commons Bentham's plan for parliamentary reform. Referring to this Westminster praise, in a later letter Bentham boasted, "I know not, as yet what may come into my mind to say to you but, for an introduction to it, whatever it may be, I will take the liberty of referring to a character [sketch] given of me the 2d of June 1818 in and as I think you will see *by*, our House of Commons." Bentham also told Bolívar of the praise he had received for his Bavarian penal code and that the authorities of Greece had asked him to draw up a "complete code of laws" which, if Bolívar could use it, Bentham would send to him as well. Once Bentham felt secure in his relations with Bolívar, he began giving him advice, offering his services, and making various requests.[3]

Bolívar reacted to Bentham's comments with the hoped for words of praise and flattery. The first letter dated September 27, 1822, is almost totally a panegyric. Bolívar apologized for the delay of his answer caused by the pressures of the fight against Spain. Then, he wrote, "But Sir, could you have conceived, that the name of the preceptor of legislators is never pronounced, even in these savage regions of America, without veneration, nor without gratitude?" He continued thanking him for the "direct com-

3. Bentham to Bolívar, January 24, 1820, in UCL, X, 3–6; Bentham to Bolívar, December 24, 1820, in UCL, CLXIII, 24; Bentham to Bolívar, January 6, 1823, in UCL, XII, 90. Bentham refers to Burdett's comments about Bentham in the debate on parliamentary reform: "Removed from the turmoil of active life, voluntarily abandoning both the emoluments and the power which it held out to dazzle ambitious and worldly minds; he has passed his days in the investigation of the most important truths." T. C. Hansard (ed.), *The Parliamentary Debates from the Year 1803 to the Present Time* (London, 1819) XXXVIII, 1131, col. 1164.

munication" which Bentham had sent "without any particular merit of my own, of a part of those sacred truths, which you have scattered over the Earth to fecundate the moral world." Then Bolívar boasted a bit of his own role in South America: "I have paid my tribute of enthusiasm to Mr. Bentham and I hope Mr. Bentham will adopt me as one of his disciples, as, in consequence of being initiated in his doctrines, I have defended liberty till it has been made the sovereign rule of Colombia." Before closing this brief letter he referred to Bentham as the geometrician of legislation with pleas "that his light may be permitted to reach even here."[4]

Probably the most pleasing correspondence of any Spanish American to Bentham was that of José del Valle. Del Valle initiated the correspondence in 1826[5] and it continued until Bentham's death. José del Valle, born in 1776 in Honduras, had been instrumental in achieving Central American independence from Spain and Mexico and had narrowly missed becoming the first president of the Central American Federation. Del Valle fit perfectly into Bentham's scheme for Spanish America and two facets of del Valle's personality made his correspondence with Bentham edifying to both. The first of these is best described in del Valle's own words in letters to Alvaro Florez Estrada: "I love Europe and those that are her beautiful savants" and "It is my desire that every savant in Europe should dedicate his talent to designing a plan that America should follow in her foreign and domestic affairs." How Bentham must have exulted in this! The second trait is assessed by Louis Bumgartner in his excellent study of del Valle: "One inescapable impression that emerges from a study of his life, before and after 1821, is that he felt that Guatemala was too provincial and thus unappreciative of his talents and that he was missing

4. Bolívar to Bentham, September 27, 1822, in UCL, X, 7.
5. Rafaél Heliodoro Valle, in his *Cartas de Bentham a José del Valle* (Mexico, 1942), inaccurately reads the draft of an extract of a letter from del Valle to Bentham printed in Bowring's edition of *Works*, XI, 71, as August 3, 1821, instead of August 3, 1831. Interestingly, the full letter of August 3, 1831, appears in *Cartas del José Cecilio del Valle*, 243–44, but Rafaél persists in his introduction that the correspondence began with a letter from del Valle to Bentham dated August 3, 1821 (p. xxxix).

fame or at least proper recognition, by reason of geography."
Through his letters to and from Bentham, the Central American
who dressed by English standards could perhaps get a savant to
give thought to Central America's problems, and, at least vicari-
ously, he could enjoy the friendship of the great of this world
which he believed was his due. For Bentham, then, here was a
willing ear to his plans and a source of ever-abundant praise.[6]

The first letter in this correspondence was from del Valle to
Bentham. It is undated, but written in the upper right-hand corner
is a note "received in 1826." Bentham's response to the first letter
requesting his assistance in drawing up a civil code for the state of
Guatemala[7] is dated November 10, 1826. Around this time, Bentham met del Valle's cousin, Prospero de Herrera, who had gone
to London to try to form a company with English capital to exploit
the Herrera mines. It was through Herrera that Bentham gained
much of his knowledge about Guatemala and through him that he
attempted to be of service to del Valle.[8]

The correspondence between Bentham and del Valle, which
came late in Bentham's life, reveals Bentham's own realization of
his advanced age. His first letter recommended the adoption of the
Livingston penal code by Guatemala "without waiting to see what,
if anything, I may be able to finish during the course of the few
days which a man who was 78 years old on the 15 February 1826
can have remaining." Thus Bentham's letters to del Valle tend to
concentrate much more on those items of great interest to Bentham: the code, government, education, and freedom of the press,
with little space devoted to the more mundane topics that he had
written of to Rivadavia and Bolívar. In a letter dated March 18,

6. Bumgartner, *José del Valle of Central America*, 258, 180, 198.
7. See Chapter Two herein for details.
8. Bumgartner, *José del Valle of Central America*, 258. Bumgartner states that it
was through Herrera that the correspondence between del Valle and Bentham began. This seems strange, for on November 10, 1826, Bentham wrote a letter to del
Valle's arch enemy, Manuel José Arce, who had become Central American president
rather than del Valle, telling him of his request from del Valle for his aid and his
willingness to help. Herrera would surely have explained this to Bentham. In his
letter of March 18, 1826, Bentham confessed to del Valle that he had written Arce
as a matter of propriety, but now he understood the situation and propriety no
longer demanded it. (UCL, XII, 382).

1827, Bentham parenthetically stated, "for being in my 80th year, the fear of dying before my . . . Code is finished is continually operating upon me as a whip to a horse."[9]

Bentham's interests were catholic, to say the least, and his correspondence with these three Spanish American leaders graphically illustrates this. The letters range from his recommendations of friends and acquaintances, to his desire to find translators for his works, to his hopes for seeing his panopticon plans adopted, to his botanical curiosity; but always there remains his love of praise and his search for recognition.

Unable to direct Spanish American development in person, Bentham recommended to both Rivadavia and Bolívar individuals whom he believed could assist them in building a functioning utilitarian government. Some of those he suggested were friends, even as close friend as John Bowring; others were persons whom he know only by reputation. Such a recommendation as the latter prompted him to initiate the correspondence which Rivadavia, then residing in Paris, had requested. Bentham suggested that Rivadavia employ Manuel Marío Cambronero and his associate, Buren, in the service of Buenos Aires. He identified Cambronero as the minister of justice in Spain under Joseph Bonaparte, who had fled to France when Joseph fell. To prove his proper credentials, Bentham noted that Cambronero "was the first who at Madrid, began to spread about Dumont's Treatise on Legislation." To further enhance his commendation he told Rivadavia that he, Rivadavia, could have no greater admirers than Cambronero and Buren of him and his works. Bentham had learned of them through his brother, Samuel, who was living in the south of France, and he promised to ask him to determine the attitude of the two Spaniards towards "Holy Independence." Rivadavia responded quickly to this letter, saying that he had heard of Combronero though not of Buren but that Bentham's word was sufficient recommendation. He hesitated, however, to take any action, saying that he would wait until the next year to pursue the matter

9. Bentham to del Valle, March 18, 1827, in UCL, XII, 355, 382.

while he better informed himself of the two. But the next letter of Bentham ended any need for that because Samuel Bentham reported to his brother that, although the two exiles were liberals, they could not support independence because of their families and their dependents. Then Bentham admitted that the recommendation was his intrigue, his alone, not his brother's or the Spaniards'.[10]

But the same letter that removed Cambronero and Buren from consideration contained two more recommendations to Rivadavia. The first one was for Charles Hammond, who was planning to establish a colony in Australia. Bentham praised him as one who although still young was experienced, judicious, and capable; he then confessed that he had the idea of suggesting to Hammond that he substitute Chile for Australia or "better still your Buenos Aires."

William Effingham Laurence was an especial favorite of Bentham if the frequency and fervency of Bentham's comments about him to Rivadavia are any gauge. In his second letter Bentham introduced Laurence in the "quality of counselor," a political counselor, whose interests were the same as those of Rivadavia. He stressed later in the letter Laurence's intense dedication to liberty, especially constitutional security and liberty of the press. In the letters examined there is no evidence that Rivadavia ever responded to these comments on either Hammond or Laurence. But this did not stop Bentham. In a long letter to Rivadavia written in 1822 after Rivadavia's return to Buenos Aires and his assumption of the position as secretary of state, Bentham again referred to Laurence, this time as "our Excellent friend William Effingham Laurence." Bentham told Rivadavia that Laurence was on his way to Australia "with a cargo of his own" but that he would probably break his trip by a stop at Rio de Janeiro. The Englishman could not resist the temptation to perhaps goad Rivadavia about his lack of encouragement of Laurence as he described Laurence by declaring that "a worthier man—a more benevolent cosmopolite—never

10. Bentham to Rivadavia, February 20, 1819, in Add. MSS 33545, BM.

left any country—very few better informed or more intelligent."[11]

In the last of the letters of Bentham to Rivadavia, Bentham returned once more to Laurence, telling the porteño that "our friend William Effingham Laurence on his way to Van Dimien land in a vessel of his own" had stopped at Rio and from there had dispatched to Rivadavia some Bentham works printed since Rivadavia left Europe. Boasting that the minister at Rio had vowed to propose that Bentham "be invited to draw up a compleat code of laws for them," he told him that the Brazilian government had urged Laurence to stay in Rio to help them. Though tempted, Laurence refused and set sail for Van Dimien land, where he had satisfactorily begun a settlement.[12]

Although many of the persons for whom Bentham hoped to find gainful employment might not have had any interest in the position, one, John Bowring, in all likelihood did. Bowring had not become acquainted with Bentham until 1820 when their common interest in Spanish affairs brought them together. He remained close to Bentham, in a proprietary and protective manner, until Bentham's death, at which time he took upon himself the task, at Bentham's request, of organizing the Bentham works for publication and writing a biography. Bentham recommended to Rivadavia that he employ Bowring as his commercial agent for the purchase of machinery in England to be used by the prisoners under Bentham's panopticon scheme which he urged Rivadavia to adopt. He was high in his praise of Bowring not only as a commercial agent, but also because "for everything else that affords a promise of usefulness to mankind Bowring would be your man, of all men I ever knew, or can hope to know." Bentham again mentioned Bowring to Rivadavia in his letter of 1824 in which he told of the death of Echeverría, Bolívar's agent in England, who might have been "coadjuster to you." He identified Bowring as "an intimate friend of mine . . . whose name, if any English newspapers ever reach you, can not be altogether unknown to you," but this time he omits the recommendation. In his correspondence with

11. *Ibid.*, 1822.
12. Bentham to Rivadavia, April 5, 1824, in UCL, XII, 269–74.

Bolívar, Bentham continued his attempt to find gainful employment for his friend as the agent of Colombia in England. (While his letters to Rivadavia that mention or recommend Bowring were written in 1822 and 1824, he wrote his letters to Bolívar on this subject in 1823.) The list of Bowring's qualifications that Bentham sent Bolívar reveals to a degree what Bentham thought a new nation dedicated to his ideas needed. The list included:

1. Knowledge of Country sent to
2. Acquaintance with character, circumstances and mode of thinking of those individuals with which agent must deal
3. Knowledge of improvements needed and means of supply
4. Knowledge of articles needed and best means of obtaining them
5. Knowledge of what articles can be produced in home country and how to develop and produce them
6. Acquaintance with beneficial and liberating institutions that might be adapted or corresponded with, such as:
   a. schools—mutual improvement type
   b. prisons
   c. societies for advancement of agriculture,—already in existence in Colombia, but proper agent can bring it into communication with those of England, Scotland, and Ireland
   d. societies for advancement of Botany and Horticulture
   e. Mineralogy and Geology—how to best develop
   f. lectures on useful branches of Art and Science, Medicine in all its branches, chemistry, Mechanics, practical mathematics, civil engineering, ship building and natural history
   g. correspondence between two nations

Bentham wrote Bolívar that if he accepted this list of qualifications as requisite for the Colombian agent in England, then an Englishman would be better suited than a Colombian. Then Bentham admitted to the Liberator that the list was actually drawn up at his request that Bowring itemize his own qualifications for the job. Bentham tried to anticipate Bolívar's objection that agents should not remain in that position for a long period of time by assuring him that replacing an agent every three years meant that each new agent, inexperienced, must come to grips with massive information, while an English agent such as Bowring would be knowledgeable and capable from the beginning.[13]

Another letter, written in June of the same year, bears a note at the top "Employed"; its title reads "J. B. to Bolivar—an Agency for Colombia—and Bowring," with the subtitle "Colombian Agents in England—their inaptitude." After an apology to Bolívar for his intrusion, Bentham told him of his "hope of rendering service to the country the destiny of which is in your hands." In his style of overstating a case, he continued by commenting that the choice of Colombia's diplomatic agents to England had "from first to last been most unfortunate." The first one, whom Bentham knew and respected, Echeverría, had died; as for the other agents of Colombia, Bentham says, "It would have been better for her had they never been born." He informed Bolívar of his responsibility to improve the reputation of Colombia in England, where it had reached a new low. "Thus, Sir, you have delivered the country from tyranny: you or nobody will deliver her from general contempt." Bentham then told Bolívar that Secretary Canning said that if Colombia did not pay her bills to various merchants in England, England would not recognize Colombia's independence. On the next page of the letter, Bentham pursued this idea, saying that he had looked for substantiating evidence of Canning's position to send to Bolívar only to discover that the information was all false. Actually, Canning had held that since the transactions were private and not acknowledged by the British government, he could not intervene in any way on the behalf of the British merchants. But after recognition, he would be most happy to enforce such claims. Bentham apologized profusely for his misstatement. The balance of the letter treated mainly the agents previously appointed: Mr. Zea, who had died; Mr. Mendy, who had been transferred to the Netherlands; and the remaining Mr. Revenga, who was in prison. Of the four agents sent by Colombia to England, two had spent considerable time in prison, Bentham reminded the Colombian leader. In this letter as found at University College, London, no

13. *Ibid.*, 388, 110–14.

mention is made in the body of the letter of Bowring as a potential agent, yet at the top of three of the four sheets appears "J. B. to Bolivar for Bowring."[14]

Bentham's suggestion of Bowring was not his first recommendation to Bolívar. Perhaps Bentham's first letter, which was not found in any of the papers examined, served as a recommendation. In Bentham's own hand there is a note that one letter to Bolívar was not sent, but another was "sent instead of it, by Mr. Hall engaged as Quarter Master General by General Devereux." In a letter dated December 24, 1820, he told Bolívar of a letter from "Mr. Francis Hall (Colonel in your Establishment I see him stiled in our newspapers) from which I receive the agreeable information of the kind reception you were pleased to give to him, and the flattering conception that it was to the letter I took the liberty of troubling you with that he considered himself as more or less indebted to you for it." Hall, of course, remained in South America writing the book on Colombia that urged immigration to that new state.[15]

Bentham made a more definite recommendation of Leander Miranda, the son of General Francisco Miranda. Evidently unaware of Bolívar's role in the capture of Francisco de Miranda,[16] Bentham on January 6, 1823, wrote a long letter, a copy of which has at the top, "J. B. to Bolivar for Miranda." Leander Miranda would personally deliver the letter, Bentham wrote, and "his name will suffice to ensure, at your hands, all such kind attentions as his disposition and acquirements may show that he is qualified to receive." The young man had asked Bentham for a letter of introduction to Bolívar because he was going to Colombia to edit a newspaper. Bentham assured Bolívar of the moral character of Leander. "In point of justice [I am] compelled to sign his certificate in the character of a disciple of my own." Indeed he and James Mill had jointly assisted Leander in his choice of books to take with him. As for his education and experience, Lady Hester Stanhope, near

14. *Ibid.*, 129–33.
15. Bentham to Bolívar, January 24, 1820, in UCL, X, 3–6; Bentham to Bolívar, December 24, 1820, in UCL, CLXIII, 23.
16. For details see Robertson, *The Life of Miranda*, II, 167–95, and Gerhard Masur, *Simón Bolívar* (Albuquerque, 1948), 90–107.

relative of Minister Pitt and a close friend of Francisco Miranda, had supported the young Miranda during a two- or three-year stay on the continent of Europe and a brief sojourn to Palestine. Bentham excused himself from not becoming earlier involved in his education by saying that Leander had been under the patronage of Nicolas Vansittart, the chancellor of the exchequer. But once he learned that Leander was going to South America, Bentham had put him "under the wing of several lawyers" who had taken him to court as an observer and introduced him to newspaper editors and other distinguished people. Bentham used this recommendation of Miranda to discuss at length his views of English education in general, saying that "had he fallen in my way a few years earlier," he would have seen that he got a more practical education. From this point on, Bentham became absorbed in Hazelwood School and other educational matters. It was not until the final postscript that he returned to Leander saying, "By all that I can learn whether from my own observations or from the observations of those who had more instructive opportunities than I have had the mind of this young man is at once judicious, steady and animated; of his active talents no means of judging have come in my way."[17]

Whether Bolívar received this letter is not clear from the Bentham-Bolívar correspondence. However, Leander Miranda did go to Colombia, where he was received by Bolívar and evidently came to hold a measure of esteem from the Liberator. O'Leary's *Memorias* contain three letters from Leander to Bolívar written from Bogotá in April, September, and October of 1829. In the first one Leander agreed to take charge of the education of Bolívar's nephew; in the second one, he enclosed articles from papers in the United States that treat the conduct of the "infamous Lancaster," the conditions of Colombia, and the reconquest of America by Spain "surely written by the Spanish expelled from Mexico." The final letter dealt with a letter to Bolívar from Henry Clay, the friendship of General Jackson for Bolívar, and the general political situation of Colombia.[18]

17. Bentham to Bolívar, January 6, 1823, in UCL, XII, 80.
18. O'Leary (ed.), *Memorias del General O'Leary*, XII, 521–26.

Bentham, keenly aware of the widespread circulation of Dumont's editions of his works in Spain and Spanish America, endeavored to find suitable translators so that his works might be of more service to these Spanish-speaking areas. When Bentham first met Rivadavia in 1818, Rivadavia told him that he was "just halfway . . . in the translation of the first of those volumes" edited by Dumont in French. Later in his first letter to Bentham, Rivadavia reported that he was making some progress in the translation of his "immortal works." Although he could not devote as much time to it as he wished, he would not abandon such an enterprise. He followed this with praise for Bentham's work which followed "the ways opened by Bacon, Locke, Newton and Smith." In his response to this in October, Bentham told Rivadavia that he had heard through his brother, Samuel, that a Don Pedro Boza de Mendoza, who had been professor of law at the University of Santiago in Galicia and a member of the Royal Academy of Public Law at Madrid, had undertaken a similar translation of "Dumont principes." However, Bentham questioned whether such a Spanish version could be published. In Spain, definitely not; in France, yes, but why? Only Buenos Aires and Chile would be truly interested in such an undertaking, Bentham argued. He suggested to Rivadavia that at this point he get in touch with Mendoza to negotiate an arrangement for the purchase of his translation paying a reasonable sum—perhaps two hundred francs—for the three volumes. With this translation settled, Rivadavia could begin work translating the *Theorie des Peines et des Recompenses* in two volumes. Bentham turned then to the problems of reaching such an agreement with Mendoza, suggesting that his brother and Cambronero and Buren might be of assistance, and promised to write immediately to his brother about it himself.

In a letter to Rivadavia in February of 1819 Bentham said that his brother reported that Mendoza had finished the translation of the three volumes, which had already been sent to a publisher in France; the published volumes were to be sent to Spain and other places. He added that the printer had appointed someone to discuss with Rivadavia the translation of all the other works of Bentham, and that such an arrangement would be pleasing to Bentham.[19]

Bentham did not discuss the translation of his works into Spanish with Bolívar and del Valle. Del Valle, in his letter to Bentham, did write of translations. In what seems to be his last letter to Bentham, he told his friend that he had announced in one of his published tracts that "if there were subscribers, I would translate all your works." Later in the same letter he informed Bentham that he was translating his pamphlet, "Official Aptitude Maximized, Expense Minimized," whose basic principle should guide his republic.[20]

Since so much of his life had been devoted to the development of the panopticon prison, it appears a bit unusual that Bentham devoted so little space in his Spanish American correspondence to it. But Bentham's interest span in some ways was at best brief, and his panopticon endeavors had lasted quite long. Indeed, if Leslie Stephen's view is accepted, Bentham was more concerned with the very nature of government than a particular solution to a problem. But in his letter to Rivadavia in 1822, he told of writing to the authorities at Colombia recommending that they establish a single panopticon style prison and employ Colonel Francis Hall, an Englishman serving with General Devereux and Bolívar, to head the project. "Being so well acquainted as you are with the *Traité de Legislation*, etc., Panopticon can scarcely be altogether out of your mind," Bentham began and continued with a review of the fate of his plan in England, due to "the personal vengeance of Geo. 3rd." He stressed that a single one be built, not the "hundreds which is what the Prison Committee of the Spanish Cortes recommended as you will see, to be done in Ultramaria as well as the Peninsula." The success of such a plan depended on the contractual status of the management which was in partnership with the government, he explained. Evidently it would produce profits "if there be any man of adequate talent and probity, whose fortune you would wish to make." To Colombia and Rivadavia Bentham

19. Bentham to Rivadavia, February 20, 1819, in Add. MSS 33545, BM.
20. Del Valle, *Cartas de José Cecilio del Valle*, 244.

offered his own services in England without charge. The significance Bentham still attached to his plan was revealed as he ended his comments on this subject: "Criminal Code may be heaped upon Criminal Code, but without such an instrument belonging to it, no tolerably efficient one will be found in countries the population of which is in the state in which yours is, and in this opinion I am far indeed from being singular."[21]

Although Bentham did not recommend his panopticon scheme in his letters to del Valle, he did advocate that he use the manifold mode of writing. In his letter commenting on federal form, Bentham suggested universal registration along with "universal publication, and communication will be established in such sort that nothing in the way of receipt and expenditure in its own concern, shall be known in any one state, without being known as soon as the post can convey it, in the seat of the central government, and in the seat of the government of every other state." The expense of such would be "reduced to a tuft by a mode of writing called the manifold mode, practiced under my eye." He promised del Valle to send more information on this early form of carbon paper duplication as well as a fairly large quantity of the materials used in it.[22]

In the same letter to Rivadavia recommending the panopticon, Bentham revealed his interest in botany. This was, he wrote, one "of the small number of useful sciences which under the Spanish domination were neither prohibited nor even I believe intentionally discouraged in Spanish Ultramaria." Should Rivadavia care to send to Bentham specimens of "the natural order of the vegetable kingdom in your republic," Bentham would "accept in that shape payment in the only shape in which I ever receive payment for any such little service as it may be in the power of my labours to render to the species of animal to which I belong."[23] There is no evidence in the Bentham manuscripts that Rivadavia ever attempted payment to his English friend in this kind.

21. Bentham to Rivadavia, June 13, and 15, 1822, in UCL, LX, 18 and XII, 387–88.
22. Bentham to del Valle, March 18, 1827, in UCL, XII, 362–63.
23. Bentham to Rivadavia, June 13 and 15, 1822, in UCL, LX, 20.

The absence of such a reply did not deter Bentham from pursuing his botanical interests. In a letter to Bolívar, dated December 24, 1820, while Bolívar was still enmeshed in armed struggle against Spain, Bentham requested that Bolívar send him roots, seeds, or plants of a vegetable called "Arrachaca." He phrased his request in this manner: "For these many years, necessity has compelled you, to a degree which you can not but deplore, to contribute to lessen the numbers of mankind: should it be in your power, at the expense of a few words, in any degree to repair the breach, they will, I flatter myself, not be grudged." At least half of the four or five million Irishmen, he continued, owed their continued existence to the root, called potato, that came from Bogotá. This other vegetable, arrachaca, was supposed to be superior even to the potato but, he added parenthetically, "I know not on what grounds." This arrachaca, which belongs to the parsley family, is similar to the parsnip but larger and fleshier.[24]

Bentham first became aware of this plant from an article in the *Morning Chronicle* of November 11, 1820. The article was in the form of "A Letter to all British Officers, and to all other Friends of Humanity in Santa fé de Bogotá, in the Kingdom of New Granada, in South America, and to all Editors of Newspapers whose papers may reach that country." The letter contained a dramatic plea to help feed the poor of the world by sending to England arrachaca plants or seeds. A footnote by the editors said that the horticultural society had made arrangements to procure the plant.[25] Bentham told Bolívar that he knew not what arrangements the society was making, but he hoped that his direct request to Bolívar would only increase the possibilities of the plant's being sent to England. The Englishman professed that he was perhaps asking too much that "the President of Colombia should, in person, stoop to pick up seeds for Britain, as the Emperor Claudius did (it is said!) to pick up cockle-shells in Britain." He hastened to add, however, that Bolívar could get someone else to actually do the work. He added, however, that if only seeds were sent, information on cultivation

24. Bentham to Bolívar, December 24, 1820, in UCL, CLXIII, 28–29.
25. The *Morning Chronicle* (London), November 11, 1820.

of the plant would be necessary. But if seeds were available, Bentham wanted them with or without directions, and he suggested Colonel Hall might enclose a few seeds in his next letter. Should the seeds arrive "the glory might be worthy the name of Bolívar" and the Royal Society of London would make him an associate. As with Rivadavia, there is no evidence that Bolívar responded to this request.

Bentham followed the activities of his Spanish American friends as closely as possible not only from their letters but also the press, particularly the *Morning Chronicle*, and the Spanish American nationals who might be in London. He was quick to commend or chastise as he agreed or disagreed with their actions. He was particularly pleased with Rivadavia's trade policies. In a long letter in June of 1822, he congratulated Rivadavia on "the magnanimity and true sense of rational as well as universal interest displayed by the putting as far as depends upon laws and treaties, all nations upon the same footing in respect of commerce." In this letter he mentioned an article that had appeared in the *Morning Chronicle* in defense of the finances and economy of Buenos Aires which he pronounced on the face of it to be satisfactory.[26]

Bentham was evidently pleased in general with Rivadavia as a functioning official. In a letter to him in 1824, he said, "Time after time accounts of your *registro* find their way into our newspapers: each time they exhibit the practices not merely of the greatest Statesman late Spanish American has produced, but alas! the only one; and . . . I have found myself confirmed by every opinion I have heard." He followed this with his recriminations about the treatment of the Spanish translation of his *Codification Proposal*, but on the final page of this letter he returned to praise: "Ah my dear Sir, could you but cut yourself into two halves and send one of them to Greece." He closed by saying that Greece suffered more from debility and depravity than even Spanish America and Rivadavia's services could help.[27]

---

26. Bentham to Rivadavia, June 13 and 15, 1822, in UCL, LX, 16 and XII, 387; June, 1822, Add. MSS 33545, BM.
27. Bentham to Rivadavia, 1824, in UCL, XII, 274.

Rivadavia always reacted favorably to Bentham's flattering comments on him and his government. In a letter of August 26, 1822, Rivadavia sent Bentham a copy of his rule for legislatures and a list of his most immediate plans closing with the comment, "in one word, to make all the advantageous alterations which the hope of your approbation has given me the strength to undertake, and will enable to execute."[28]

The correspondence found in the University College, London, and British Museum collections ended in April of 1824, but this did not end the relationship between Rivadavia and Bentham. In his letter of September 21, 1824, to the legislative assembly of Greece which accompanied Rivadavia's rule for the Chamber of Deputies, he remarked, "It is now about a fortnight since I have the unlooked-for satisfaction of clasping him in my arms here in London, where he is come on some business, still governing, however, by the pupils which he has formed, and the reputation which he has acquired." He went on to say that only Buenos Aires of all Spanish and Portuguese America "has taken a firm and happy footing" and Rivadavia was its founder.[29]

Bowring stated in his biography that "of the representatives of South America in this country, Rivadavia was the man of whom Bentham thought the most highly."[30] But something happened to change the evidently warm relationship. In a letter to Bolívar in 1825 Bentham commented that only the intervention of the British government could have caused the rupture between himself and Rivadavia. In describing Rivadavia's visit to him in 1824, he mentioned the porteño's translation of James Mill's book on political economy and said that, although Mill had dined with Rivadavia in Bentham's garden, Rivadavia "never manifested the least desire to see" Bentham. He told Bolívar that he had heard that Rivadavia frequently saw British functionaries and that he had no doubt that the foreign ministry demanded the promise that Rivadavia would no longer "continue his relations with me." Bentham

28. Rivadavia to Bentham, August 26, 1822, in Add. MSS 33545, BM; Bowring (ed.), *Works*, IV, 592–93.

29. Bowring (ed.), *Works*, IV, 584.

30. *Ibid.*, X, 500.

said that he could not understand the official British attitude because, as far as commercial relations with Buenos Aires were concerned, he could not suggest any course other than the present one. But he added they could have no knowledge of this. Finally, however, Bentham revealed the hurt caused by the abandonment of a favored disciple as he remarked to Bolívar, "And I respect Rivadavia, although there is something in his temperament/nature that does not agree with the sociability of mine." Even so, he continued to recommend that Bolívar observe what Buenos Aires was doing.[31]

Materials as well as advice went out to Bolívar from the Sage of Westminster. Many of the materials Bolívar never received, but he did receive "a catechism of economics which so impressed Bolívar that he immediately ordered it translated into Spanish so that others might gain from it." In another letter, Bentham mentioned "your own children of all colours," about whose ability to go alone he says he is not capable to have a judgment. He did, however, in a later letter say that by Bolívar's simple act of abolition of slavery "more service was done to the pecuniary credit than could have been done by an arrangement of finance."[32]

Dumont's edition of Bentham's works, more so than Bentham himself, became involved in a bitter internecine fight between Bolívar and his vice president, Francisco de Paula Santander. On March 12, 1828, Bolívar issued a decree, the first article of which read "In none of the Universities of Colombia will Bentham's treatises of Legislation be taught, Article 168 of the general plan of studies being consequently changed."[33]

Bowring, in his biography of Bentham, stated, "In the year 1826, when Bolívar, who had been a correspondent of Bentham, took to his despotic course, his tampering with the rights of rep-

31. O'Leary (ed.), *Memorias del General O'Leary*, IX, 276–79. The first part of this long letter from Bentham to Bolívar is also found in UCL, XII, 335–44.

32. Lecuna (ed.), *Cartas del Libertador*, VI, 155–56; Bentham to Bolívar, December 24, 1820 and July 14, 1825, in UCL, CLXIII, 26 and XII, 210.

33. A good discussion of this is found in Armando Rojas, "La Batalla de Bentham en Colombia," *Revista de historia de América*, XXIX (1950), 37–66; the decree of Bolívar is found on page 51.

resentation, and his overthrow of the liberty of the press, he prohibited the use of Bentham's writings in the Colombia seminaries
of Education." Bowring's date was probably inaccurate, however,
for the *Cartas de Libertador* contains from the rough draft a letter
from Bolívar to Bentham in two parts, dated January, 1827. In
both parts he continued his words of praise and flattery.[34] Later in
his work, Bowring recounted a conversation with Bentham.

B— (General) Bolivar wrote to me very flattering letters. He said I had
reduced matters of legislation to mathematical certainty. I introduced
Hall to him when he went to Colombia, and Bolivar made him a colonel.

But are you aware that Bolivar has prohibited your writings? Their liberal principles are hostile to his despotic designs.

According to Bentham, Bolívar feared the power of Bentham's
ideas.

B— His despotism cannot tolerate the greatest-happiness principle. He
must put the judge out of the way before whose tribunal he trembles—
and unhappily he has power to do so. Bonaparte was in the same state of
mind. Talleyrand put into his hand, one afternoon, the Traités de Legislation: Next morning it was returned to him, and Buonaparte [*sic*] said,—
"Ah! C'est un ouvrage de genie"—'Tis a work of genius;' but never, as far
as I know did he mention it again: indeed it could not answer his purposes.[35]

Seemingly then, Bentham felt that Bolívar had abandoned utilitarian principles because they did not serve his own purposes, or
perhaps sinister interests.

While Bentham took offense at the loss of this powerful disciple, he was however, somewhat comforted by the adherence to his
ideas of Santander, who later visited him at Queen Square Place.
And del Valle's letters to Bentham were laden with praise from the
first reference to "the glorious title of legislator of the world" to
the final tribute:

34. Bowring (ed.), *Works*, X, 552; Lecuna (ed.), *Cartas*, VI, 154–56.
35. Bowring (ed.), *Works*, X, 565.

I desire that your luminous principles circulate in the new world as they do in the old. Already it begins to be published that it is necessary to reform the Constitution of this Republic. This opinion is making progress, and when reform is discussed, I do not doubt that your theories will be presented. The political world is in movement; all the states desire to improve their laws, and you have pointed out the line by which they ought to march in order not to be devoured by anarchy, nor destroyed by despotism.[36]

Bentham reacted warmly to such sentiments and he treasured del Valle's devotion and loyalty during these last years when Bolívar and Rivadavia had long since severed the bonds of friendship. Bentham published his first letter from del Valle in its original Spanish with an English translation in his *Codification Proposal*. And in a lengthy letter to Rammohum Rey in 1828, he spoke of del Valle as "the instructor of his country; such an one as you of yours. . . . I hear him spoken of, from various quarters, as by far the most estimable man that late Spanish America has produced." Bentham volunteered to forward to del Valle anything that Rey might want to send him and briefly told Rey that del Valle's political position in Guatemala was at present unsure but that "as far as I can learn, that of del Valle is most likely to be ultimately prevailing."[37] In a letter to Lafayette, Bentham was effusive in his view of del Valle: "In del Valle I behold a rising sun, by whom from its center all late Spanish America will if he lasts be illuminated."[38] Del Valle's letter of April 18, 1827, in which he discussed the need of new codes for Guatemala so pleased Bentham that he had a translation of the letter published in the *Morning Chronicle*. The heading of the article simply identified del Valle as "of Guatemala." In Bentham's papers the clipping of the article has "President" inserted.[39]

Del Valle, who seemed to understand and appreciate Bentham and his Spanish American dreams perhaps more than the other two correspondents, was sorely grieved by Bentham's death. In a

36. Del Valle to Bentham, April 18, 1827, in UCL, XII, 346.
37. Bowring (ed.), *Works*, IV, 593, 591.
38. Bentham to Marquis de Lafayette, January 17, 1827, in UCL, XII, 373.
39. Del Valle to John Bowring, January 2, 1833, in Add. MSS 33546, BM.

letter to John Bowring dated January 2, 1833, del Valle described his sadness at the loss of "a Friend, dear and Honorable." He determined, upon hearing of Bentham's passing, to make sure that Central America, if not all Spanish America, paid proper respect to its benefactor. He introduced a resolution to the congress of the Central American Republic requesting its members "appear in mourning to express the just sentiments that the death of a wise man ought to inspire."[40]

Del Valle's resolution revealed in high relief his desire to identify with the great of this world. He began with an account of Mirabeau's speech to the French Assembly at the death of Benjamin Franklin in which Mirabeau proposed that the assembly properly mourn the passing of the great American. He continued, "At the death of the European who has worked for the emancipation and legislation of all America, will the Congress of Central America not observe similar mourning?"[41] The request was immediately granted and September 1, 1832, was set aside as a day of mourning for the passing "of the illustrious defender of the independence of the colonies." The Supreme Court upon hearing of this congressional resolution voted to join them in this action.[42]

Two weeks before del Valle's resolution was published in the *Gaceta*, the news of Bentham's death had been announced there on September 3, 1832. This article briefly reviewed Bentham's life and virtually begged that in Central America Bentham's Spanish American dreams of a utilitarian utopia might become reality: "Central-American, let us venerate the memory of this benefactor of humanity . . . that the luminious principles that he had irrevocably established by means of his works, may preside in our assemblies, governments, and tribunals, and thus we will build our happiness upon indestructable foundations." The final paragraphs of this memoria told of Bentham's correspondence with José del Valle and continued, "With infinite pleasure we have seen in the

40. Del Valle, *Cartas de José Cecilio del Valle*, 253. This letter is the first one in Capitulo XII, "Correspondencia con Monsieur Julien, Director de la Reveu Encyclopedique."

41. *Gaceta Federal* (Guatemala), September 17, 1832.

42. *Ibid.*

will of Bentham, the name of this distinguished Central-American, among those of the very great men of Europe, to whom Bentham has bequeathed a ring with his picture and hair from his head, in token of friendship and esteem."[43]

Bentham's bequest of a ring with his picture and hair from his head greatly pleased del Valle and he begged Bowring to fulfill Bentham's wish by sending them. Del Valle suggested that Bowring, if he could find no other safe means of sending it, give it to Señor Murfi, who was living in London, so that he might deliver it to his correspondent, Señor Mateu, who lived in Guatemala City.[44] Evidently del Valle's plea fell on deaf ears, and he died on March 2, 1834, without ever receiving his gift. In a letter from Paris dated May 25, 1843, to del Valle's wife, Auguste Mabelin wrote that he had fulfilled her request made of him before leaving Guatemala City. He had received from Bowring, he reported, "the small box which I have not opened" that contained Bentham's legacy to her husband. Mabelin in turn had sent it to Georges Viteri, the bishop of San Salvador, who assured him of his pleasure in forwarding the box to her with punctuality.[45]

43. *Ibid.*, September 3, 1832.
44. Del Valle, *Cartas de José Cecilio del Valle*, 253.
45. *Ibid.*, 254.

Nine

CONCLUSIONS

IT IS A MATTER OF HISTORICAL FACT that the utilitarian utopia for which Bentham planned never became reality. Was it then nothing more than an old man's dream of glory? Leaving aside the allocation of influence, it can be said that many of the procedures, methods, and institutions advocated by Bentham for Spanish America became cardinal principles in the programs proposed by Spanish American liberal leaders in the first generation of independence.[1] Where and when such ideas first entered the intellectual history of the area is difficult to impossible to determine. Few ideas, after all, are totally original. It was Bentham's organization of these around his own principle of utility that gave his plan its uniqueness.

Many of the institutions that Bentham supported so vehemently were tried in Spanish America. All of the nations adopted republican forms; they drew up comprehensive, well-defined constitutions; they developed new codes to replace the old Spanish ones; under the liberals, many adopted quite extensive freedom-of-the-press laws; they put their faith in the system of teaching advocated by Lancaster; they built libraries and sustained a tremendous faith in the power of education. Bentham had foreseen

1. Jaime Rodríguez in *The Emergence of Spanish America* argues forcefully that early Spanish American liberals found their inspiration not in England, France, or the United States but from Spanish liberalism which "profoundly influenced" them (page ix).

stability, growth, achievement, and liberty. Yet the millennium failed to arrive. Why?

Perhaps one reason could be Bentham's faith in the political solution to all problems. All of the plans, laws, recommendations and advice he so freely gave to his Ultramarian friends were predicated on his basic premise, man's rationality; and the key to man's problems was the properly structured government, one based on the utilitarian maxim of providing the greatest happiness to the greatest number.

His suggestions for the adoption of a comprehensive code and for establishing republican governments naturally emphasized the political aspects. But the arguments he used in the long letters to the Spanish people urging their voluntary emancipation of their New World empire centered upon the violence done by ownership of colonies to the liberal foundations of the Spanish Constitution of 1812.

Liberty of the press, which is so frequently viewed as a civil liberty second only in importance to freedom of speech, had in Bentham's view as its primary function the assurance of the right of political criticism along with the dissemination of information. Thus the press, un-engrossed, was to keep the government honest by not only publishing information but also by acting as a public forum for all those who wished to criticize or comment on the actions of government. Through comments from citizens in the press, officials could gauge the support or opposition to their programs and gain insight into the needs and desires for new ones. The press then was to act not only as a forum but also as a lobby for the people.

Although Bentham in his Junctiana Canal plan discussed the economic advantages of such an undertaking, once more his major emphasis was political. Believing that a canal was inevitable there, he sought to eliminate the possible building of rival canals by Colombia and Mexico as well as the rivalry and animosity that might occur should one of these states build a canal alone. The land ceded by these nations was to go to the United States because its government was already based on the utilitarian maxim. Then

Mexico and Colombia would benefit as Junctiana flourished and became "a Common School, established under the eyes of both of them, an all comprehensive School, of everything that is useful in art and science, but more particularly of those things that are most useful, *good legislation, good judicature, good government* in every line"[2] (italics mine).

Bentham's suggestions in the field of education were likewise laden with political aims, for, to him, the basic purpose of education was to produce an enlightened citizenry. This required, as he saw it, the production of a literate population, the forming of the public mind, and the proper education of political leaders. In his Spanish American documents, he recommended that the Lancaster method be employed to achieve the first and help with the second, while properly filled libraries would complete the task. Schools based on the Hazelwood model would accomplish the third.

In the political emphasis Bentham gave to his Spanish American work, he virtually ignored the great mass of Indians that were actually in the majority in many of those states. His one comment on them in these documents came in an 1821 "Rid Yourselves of Ultramaria" letter when, in discussing colonial representation in the Spanish Cortes, he admitted, "True, from the Spanish population in Ultramaria, the Aborigines are to be deducted."[3] In no document did Bentham concern himself with the problem of integrating them into the national scheme—politically, economically, or socially. He seemingly disregarded their very existence, perhaps believing that if his ideas were put into practice there would be no problem with the Indians, for in a government devoted to the greatest happiness to the greatest number (and they constituted in many countries the greatest number), they would be absorbed into national life as a matter of course. Perhaps he thought that the key lay in education, that it would facilitate acculturation. But he gave no clues as to how this would be achieved.

2. "Junctiana Proposal," 1822, in UCL, CVI, 284.
3. "Rid Yourselves," 1821, 1822, in UCL, VIII, 81.

Bentham failed to see what liberal leaders who attempted to put many of the ideas he had advocated into practice soon learned. Having well-structured constitutions, codes, and carefully worded laws does not bring obedience to any of them. Liberty of the press could become license; faith in education was fine, but where were the resources to establish and sustain such an expensive endeavor? Bentham's failure to see the necessity of gaining the support or control, one way or another, over the elites of Latin America doomed his program to failure. Nowhere does Bentham concern himself with the problems of the Church, both economic and political; nowhere does he concern himself with the problems of latifundia and the landholding aristocracy; nowhere does he concern himself with the control of the army—the army that had, it felt, given its all to the cause of independence and looked to its government for its share of the spoils. By totally ignoring these three groups, Bentham ignored those elements that would bring down liberal governments wherever they were tried. The safeguards that Bentham thought were built in to protect the interests of the subject many did not work. In Spanish America the sinister interests of the ruling few consistently won out.

Perhaps in reality the early liberal leaders tried too hard to achieve Bentham's goals whether intentionally or not. Perhaps they took Bentham and his ideas too literally. Perhaps they, too, believed with Bentham that national customs, conditions, and life-styles had no bearing on the solutions of problems, that the proper laws would in time create the proper institutions. Rivadavia, for example, on August 19, 1821, as minister of state in Buenos Aires, proclaimed universal manhood suffrage to all males twenty years or older. This unlimited suffrage was in a state with monumental illiteracy, virtually no previous electoral experience, and no previous opportunity for "forming the public mind."[4] One wonders if he misunderstood Bentham on the necessity of literacy. In any case, Bentham's ideas and those of his Spanish American friends failed to develop those infant countries into well-governed

---

4. *Registro oficial, libro primero* (Buenos Aires, 1821), 18–19.

nations. Bentham's plans, after all, did not grow out of the problems of Spanish America. When transplanted there, they became almost all form with little substance.

What then can be said of Bentham and his New World Utopia? Bentham, if he did not furnish them with original ideas, did encourage early liberal leaders to experiment with these new forms. For young, struggling nations, the interest of a world-famous philosopher was edifying to say the least. Spanish Americans in return supplied his ego with accolades of interest, praise, and flattery. The communication between the Light of Westminster and the struggling Spanish Americans was sufficient unto itself.

BIBLIOGRAPHY

Books and Parts of Books

Arrowsmith, Aaron. *Atlas to Thompson's Alcedo: Dictionary of America and West Indies.* London: G. Smeeton, 1816.

Benson, Nettie L., ed. *Mexico and the Spanish Cortes, 1810–1822.* Austin: University of Texas, 1966.

Bentham, Jeremy. *Codification Proposal, addressed by Jeremy Bentham to all Nations Professing Liberal Opinions.* London: J. McCreery, 1822.

———. *Supplement to the Codification Proposal. Part II.* London: J. McCreery, n.d.

Bowring, John, ed. *The Works of Jeremy Bentham.* Vols. II, X, XI, IV. New York: Russell and Russell, 1962.

Bumgartner, Louis E. *José del Valle of Central America.* Durham: Duke University Press, 1963.

Collier, Simon. *Ideas and Politics of Chilean Independence, 1808–1833.* Cambridge: Cambridge University Press, 1967.

Dávila, Vicente *et al.*, eds. *Archivo del General Miranda.* Vols. XXI and XXII. La Habana: Editorial Lex, 1950.

Davis, Matthew L., ed. *The Private Journal of Aaron Burr.* Vol. I. New York: Harper and Brothers, 1838.

Dictionary of National Biography. Vols. II, XI. London: Oxford University Press, 1921–1922.

Duval, Miles P., Jr. *Cadiz to Cathay.* Palo Alto: Stanford University Press, 1947.

Hale, Charles A. *Mexican Liberalism in the Age of Mora, 1821–1853.* New Haven: Yale University Press, 1968.

Halévy, Elie. *The Growth of Philosophic Radicalism.* Boston: Beacon Press, 1966.

Hall, Francis. *Colombia: Its Present State and Inducements to Emigration.* London: Baldwin, Cradock and Joy, 1824.

Hansard, T. C., ed. *The Parliamentary Debates from the Year 1803 to the Present Time.* Vol. XXXVIII. London: Wyman, 1819.

Lecuna, Vicente, ed. *Cartas del Libertador.* Vol. VI. Caracas: Lit. y. Tys. del Comercio, 1929.

Lovett, Gabriel H. *Napoleon and the Birth of Modern Spain.* Vol. II. New York: New York University Press, 1965.

Manning, D. J. *The Mind of Jeremy Bentham.* London: Longmans, Green and Co., 1968.

Masur, Gerhard. *Simón Bolívar.* Albuquerque: University of New Mexico Press, 1948.

Milne, A. Taylor, ed. *Catalogue of the Manuscripts of Jeremy Bentham in the Library of University College, London.* London: Athlone, 1962.

Nocedal, Candido *et al.*, eds. *Obras de Don Gaspar Melchor de Jovellanos.* Vol. II. Madrid: M. Rivadencyra, 1859.

O'Leary, Simon B. *Memorias del General O'Leary.* Vols. XII, IX. Caracas: Gaceta Oficial, 1880.

Robertson, William Spence. *The Life of Miranda.* Vols. I, II. Chapel Hill: University of North Carolina Press, 1929.

Robinson, William Davis. *Memoirs of the Mexican Revolution.* Vol. II. London: Lackington, Hughes, Harding, Mavor & Lepard, 1821.

Rodríguez, Jaime. *The Emergence of Spanish America.* Berkeley: University of California Press, 1975.

Rodríguez, Mario. *The Livingston Codes in the Guatemalan Crisis of 1837–1838.* New Orleans: Middle American Research Institute, 1955.

Serra, A. Padilla. *Constituciones y Leyes Fundamentales de España (1808–1947).* Granada: Universidad de Granada, 1954.

Simon, Brian. *Studies in the History of Education, 1780–1870.* London: Laurence & Wishart, 1960.

Stephen, Leslie. *The English Utilitarians.* Vol. I. New York: Augustus Kelley, 1968 [1900].

Valle, Rafael Heliodoro, ed. *Cartas de Bentham a José del Valle.* Mexico: Editorial Cultura, 1942.

del Valle, José Cecilio. *Cartas de José Cecilio del Valle.* Tegucigalpa: Universidad Nacional Autonoma de Honduras, 1963.

Articles

"Lettre aux Espanols Americains, Par un de leur Compatriotes." *Edinburgh Review,* XIII (October 1808–January 1809), 277–311.

Rojas, Armando. "La Batalla de Bentham en Colombia." *Revista de historia de América,* XXIX (1950), 37–66.

Newspapers

Morning Chronicle (London), 1820, 1822.

Gaceta Federal (Guatemala), 1832.

Registro oficial, libro primero (Buenos Aires), Empiega en el mes de Septiembre de 1821 y Acaba de Diciembre del Mismo Año, 18–19.

Manuscripts

British Museum
    Jeremy Bentham Manuscripts
    Additional Manuscripts 33545, 33546, 33551, 33563
Kings College, Cambridge University
    Jeremy Bentham Manuscripts
University College, London
    Jeremy Bentham Manuscripts

  VIII. Emancipation Spanish
      J. B. to Spain: Emancipate your colonies
      Emancipation Spanish
      Rid Yourselves of Ultramaria, 1820
      Rid Yourselves of Ultramaria; being the advice of Jeremy Bentham, as given in a series of letters to the Spanish people, 1821, 1822

    IX. Correspondence, 1784–1828
     X. Correspondence—general and French, 1795–1824
   XII. Venezuela
      Caracas Necessity of an all-comprehensive Code 1810 Correspondence—United States of America, Colombia, Peru, Egypt, Greece, Guatemala; 1817–1825
   XXI. J. B.'s [illeg.] for Caracas Code
      Venezuela—Advantages from English Birth and Education
      Venezuela—Proposed law for securing the liberty of the Press, 1810
      Caracas—constitutional legislation on the evils of change, intended for Caracas on the occasion of General Miranda's Expedition; 1810, 1824
      Guatemala—Collectanea; 1823–1826
      Guatemala—Memoranda; 1827
  XXVI. Proposed law for the establishment of the liberty of the press in Venezuela; 1808
    LX. Mexico and Vera Cruz—Information from Guía de Commerciantes; 1808
      Buenos Aires—Collectanea and Correspondence; 1818–1824
      Chile—J. B. to O'Higgins; 1821
      Colombia—Simón Bolívar to E. Blaquiere (translation); 1822
      Guatemala—Memoranda; 1823
   CVI. Junctiana proposal [Nicaragua Canal]; 1822, 1823

CIX.   [Parliamentary reform]—Mexico [extracts from *Morning Chronicle* and *Traveller*]; 1821, 1822

CLXII.   Emancipation Spanish—Summary of a work, intituled "Emancipate your colonies, in a letter from Philo-Hispanus to the Spanish people"; 1820

CLXIII. Private correspondence; 1800–1826

CLXIV.   Emancipation Spanish—Introduction; 1820
         Emancipation Spanish—Corruptive influence; 1820

CLXVII. Rid yourselves of ultramaria—
         Part I, Letters 5–9; 1820–1822
         Part I, Letters 10–13; 1820–1822
         Part II, Letters 11–17; 1820–1822
         Part II, Letter 27; 1820–1821

INDEX